9/8/2019

To Cara,

Happy Birthday!

love Carmelita

Jason and Clare

xx

CAMINO FOOTSTEPS

CAMINO FOOTSTEPS
Reflections on a journey to Santiago de Compostela
Kim and Malcolm Wells

May our book give inspiration
to all those who wish to walk the
Way of St James and enjoyment to those
who can share our special experience

Many thanks to our family and friends for their great
support and encouragement. Special thanks to Anne,
Stephanie, Anita and the staff at Fremantle Press.

CONTENTS

Map of our journey	8
Introduction	11
History of the Camino	13
St James — the martyr who inspired the Camino	14
Our journey	
St Jean Pied de Port	16
The Scallop Shell and Waymarkers	28
To Orisson	30
To Burguete	34
To Zubiri	46
To Pamplona	50
To Puente La Reina	54
To Estella	62
To Los Arcos	68
To Logroño and Burgos	80
To León	85
To O'Cebreiro	96
To Triacastela	100
To Sarria	106
To Portomarín	116
To Palas de Rei	124
To Arzúa	130
To Arca	138
Santiago de Compostela	141
Final reflections	162
Planning and photography hints	164

MAP OF OUR JOURNEY

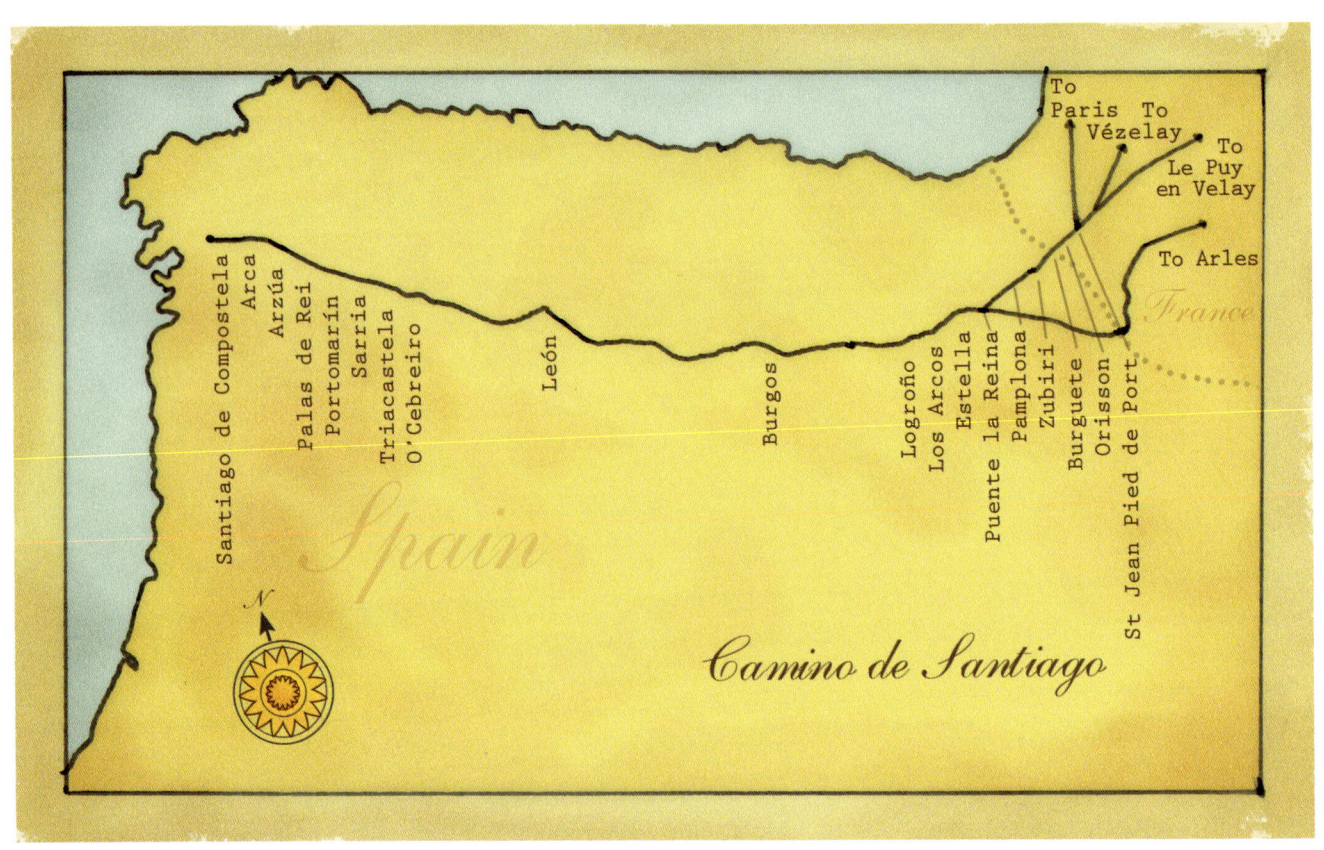

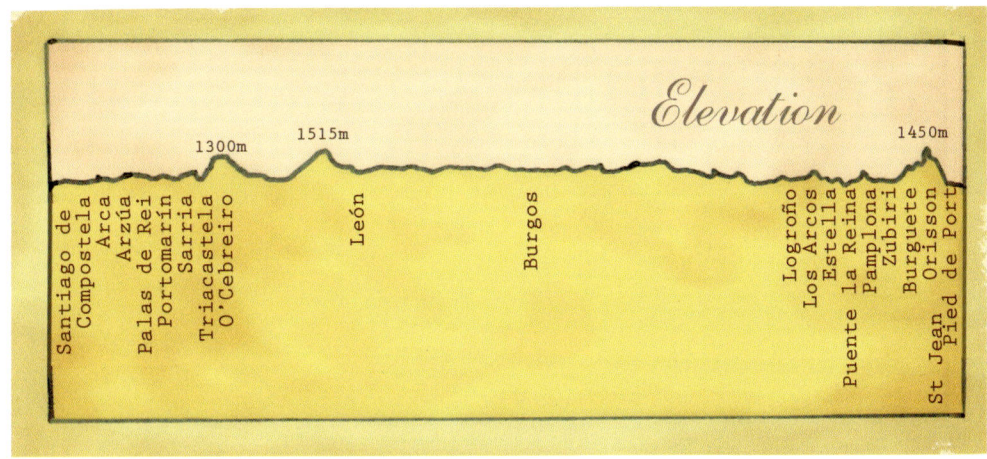

The Camino de Santiago, from St Jean Pied de Port to Santiago de Compostela, is a journey of 798 km, divided into 34 days averaging 24 km per day. Four main French pilgrim routes — from Paris, Vézelay, Le Puy en Velay and Arles — converge into this route in the Pyrenees, three at St Jean Pied de Port.

Our journey covered 332 km divided into two sections with additional stopovers at Burgos and León.

The elevation profile of the Camino de Santiago gives some idea of the terrain. There is a real test of endurance on Day 2, crossing the Col de Lepoeder at 1450 m. Between Burgos and León there is a long section as the route crosses the *meseta* (plains) offering little shade and water. After León, hills reappear once more, becoming mountainous approaching the highest point of 1515 m on Day 25 — by which time, hopefully, the fitness levels should have improved — and again coming into O'Cebreiro.

INTRODUCTION

The Camino de Santiago, also known as the Camino Francés and the Way of St James, is a route from St Jean Pied de Port to Santiago de Compostela covering a distance of 798 km and taking 34 walking days if an extra overnight stop is made at Orisson in the Pyrenees.

We decided to limit our journey to 332 km and divided our walk into two sections: from St Jean Pied de Port to Logroño (163 km over 8 days), and from Pedrafita near O'Cebreiro to Santiago (169 km over 7 days).

Our walk took us into the most varied countryside; through old forests, beautiful valleys and farmland, crossing winding streams, meandering in and out of old farming hamlets and delightful villages, climbing mountains and descending onto plains.

Travelling by bus over the flat, dry middle section of the *meseta* (plains), we followed much of the Camino route, stopping to explore the old cathedral cities of Burgos for two days, and León for three days.

Additionally, we spent three days in St Jean before commencing our walk and another four days in Santiago when we finished. Having a stopover at each end of the Camino was most welcome: it allowed us time to prepare mentally for what was ahead, and to absorb the special moment of arriving at our destination after a journey totalling 27 days.

We also discovered that there were many ways to cross the Camino de Santiago. We met walkers who chose an arranged self-guided program, walking sections such as ours but having their accommodation pre-booked and their backpacks taken on ahead each day. Many European walkers opted to walk shorter sections, taking years to complete the route.

There were individual groups with 'skippers' taking turns to drive ahead, book accommodation and carry the luggage for those who walked. Others were part of guided groups who combined travelling by bus with walking. We also met guided groups on gourmet or historical tours.

Some pilgrims chose self-guided or guided tours by bicycle. Others travelled the Way by donkey or horse.

The Camino becomes a moving caravan of people heading to Santiago in different ways along an ancient path walked by tens of thousands of pilgrims since medieval times. Just to touch the old stone of the buildings and bridges, to walk the path built over the centuries, to see the variety of architectural styles, from Roman and Moorish to medieval to Gothic and Renaissance — brings to life the history of the Way, and for us becomes powerfully spiritual.

It was also the pilgrims we met who made the whole experience so wonderful, each one undertaking the walk for their own reasons. We came from different countries, spoke different languages, yet all of us were in some way walking together, bonded by peace and friendship.

It was very moving when we finally reached our goal, the Santiago Cathedral, the resting place of the relics of the Apostle James. We felt a sadness in our hearts because our walk was completed. However, we knew it was a special part of our ongoing journey, an inspirational experience.

THE HISTORY OF THE CAMINO

Before its existence as a Christian pilgrimage, the present Camino is also believed to have significance for the ancient pagan peoples of the Iberian Peninsula, among them the Celts. One legend has it that walking the route was a pagan fertility ritual and the scallop shell was a symbol of fertility, rebirth and rejuvenation (in the Middle Ages the scallop shell reappeared as a symbol worn by pilgrims who successfully reached Santiago). Later the Romans, who conquered Spain around 200 BC, occupied its westernmost point, Cape Finisterre (literally 'the end of the world' or 'Land's End' in Latin).

The original Camino through Spain was heavily travelled from the Middle Ages — the first record of its being used by pilgrims (*peregrinos*) from Eastern Europe, the Nordic countries, Turkey, the Adriatic, France, Portugal and England was in the 9th century. It was restored in the 11th century by Sancho III the Great of Navarre. From the early 12th century the pilgrimage was also made by bishops, kings and the rich of the time, with St Francis of Assisi himself making a pilgrimage.

There is a record (the *Codex Calixtinus*) of the route taken by Picaud, the cleric from Parthenan-le-Vieux, written in about 1139. He mentions the pilgrims' hospitals, places of refuge (*refugios* or *albergues*) and even the quality of the food and drinking water on the journey. These establishments had royal protection and were a lucrative source of revenue for the towns and villages along the Way.

A Papal decree by Pope Calixto II granting Compostela 'Holy Year' status was made in the 11th century. This allowed pilgrims who visited Santiago Cathedral during such years to receive a plenary indulgence — a full remission of sins. El Año Santo (Holy Year) is celebrated when Apostles' Day, July 25, falls on a Sunday, usually every five years.

The Pilgrims' Office in Santiago records the number of pilgrims each year who present their stamped passports as evidence of walking the minimum 100 km (or riding 200 km) on the Way of St James — this is the compulsory distance required to obtain a Compostela Certificate. Between 1986 and 2005 a total of 938,728 pilgrims received a Compostela Certificate. In 1986 there were 2,491 pilgrims, 2003 showed a huge increase to 74,614 and in 2004 this rose to 179,944, due to it being a Holy Year. In 2006, by October approximately 95,000 pilgrims were registered to receive a Compostela Certificate.

Approximately 20% of all recorded pilgrims are bike riders. Interestingly, statistics kept on ages of those who walk or ride the Camino reveal that Malcolm falls into the 1% of those over 70 years of age. He was really chuffed about this, and at the same time could not understand why more of his peers are not experiencing the Camino. (Two years on we are about to embark on another Camino, the pilgrim's route from Le Puy en Velay in France, finishing in the wonderful Pyrenees town of St John Pied de Port from where this walk commenced.)

In 1993 UNESCO declared the Camino de Santiago a world heritage site.

ST JAMES the martyr who inspired the Camino

Scenes from the life of St James the Apostle depicting his voyage to Santiago de Compostela, his preaching to the pagans, his trial by King Herod, his beheading, and the return of his body to Santiago by boat.

It was shortly after Christ's crucifixion that James, one of His twelve Apostles, sailed to the Spanish region of Galicia, near where Santiago is today. He wanted to preach the Christian faith to the pagan population, and after years of limited success, he returned to Jerusalem in 42 AD.

By the order of King Herod Agrippa, James was beheaded. His followers brought his martyred body back by boat to what is now known as Santiago de Compostela.

Records from 1110 document that in 815 a hermit named Pelayo saw lights glimmering near his home, which were also seen by some peasants. The local Bishop, Theodomirus, was informed and in the forest he found a tomb, guarded by marble stones, in which lay the remains of the Apostle James. The name originally given to this burial site was Campus Stellae, meaning, 'the field of the star'.

The Asturian King Alfonso II built a small church over the tomb, and later a Benedictine monastery was built there. The monks were entrusted with guarding the tomb and still do so today at the magnificent Santiago Cathedral. The building of the cathedral was begun in 1075 and additions and alterations were made from 1211 to 1506.

Over the centuries, Santiago, like Rome and Jerusalem, has become one of the most important Christian holy places. Since the 12th century tens of thousands of pilgrims from all over Europe have walked the path called Camino de Santiago. Many churches, monasteries, hospitals and inns were built to serve the pilgrims' needs. In some sections the path follows remnants of an ancient Roman road and crosses many Roman bridges, which are still intact today.

Present-day pilgrims walk the Camino de Santiago for many reasons — some for personal or religious enlightenment, some as a historical and cultural journey, others for its physical challenge or as tourists; most, however, are touched by its powerful spirituality.

ST JEAN PIED DE PORT

A fast TVG train from Paris delivers us quickly to Bayonne, where we board a slower regional train to St Jean Pied de Port. Compared to the sleek TVG which speeds through the countryside so fast that it blurs the vision of anything seen close by, the local train chugs along, allowing its occupants to take in all it passes. Sounds and smells drift through the open windows, pervading the old wooden cabins. Travelling slowly along a winding route we are mesmerised by the lush green Basque Pyrenees valleys, the clear rushing streams, the white farmhouses and small hamlets built in a style usually seen in the Swiss Alps. It is all so beautiful.

We meet other walkers in the train's few carriages. Hardly able to contain our excitement about reaching St Jean and commencing our journey, there is a lot of changing seats, talk and plans to meet again either in St Jean or on the Way. We arrive at the rather unkempt and deserted provincial railway station and step down into a new adventure. With our packs on our backs we make our way up a steep hill towards the old quarter of the town.

In the French Pyrenees, only 8 km from the Spanish border, St Jean stands at the base of the Roncesvalles Pass, which has traditionally been an important crossing point into Spain for those beginning their pilgrimage to Santiago de Compostela. It offers a place to rest and reflect before embarking on the arduous mountain crossing and the 798 km journey ahead.

It also allows time to repack backpacks and send ahead any surplus baggage to the Santiago Post Office. We found this service reliable and invaluable as it is essential to minimise the weight being carried. In our case we sent on 6 kg of extra luggage in a box supplied by the local post office.

Pilgrims are immersed in the fortified town's ancient history as soon as they enter through the 15th-century Porte St Jacques (St James' Gate), following the footsteps of the thousands of fellow pilgrims who have taken this route.

Many of the buildings in the old town date from the 16th and 17th centuries, and are made of the softest pink and grey schist. The 14th-century Gothic church of Nôtre Dame du Bout du Pont (Church of Our Lady by the Bridge End) is a deeper reddish hue.

Accommodation and restaurants abound, as do craft shops displaying colourful traditional Basque linen. On market day, usually a Monday, the region's produce is sold.

There is a fairytale feeling about St Jean. It is so pretty and so ancient; like a history book, in which the old fortifications and buildings are the pages. The town, overshadowed by the Citadel, surrounded and protected by the fortified walls, is reflected in the bubbling, clear River Nive.

Within the simple and tranquil 14th-century Nôtre Dame du Bout du Pont, pilgrims can contemplate their approaching journey, settle their thoughts and prepare for what is ahead — for the journey is not only outward, it is also an inward journey.

A narrow cobbled street meanders down the hill from the Porte St Jacques (St James' Gate), flanked by beautifully preserved stone buildings whose windows are decorated with intricately laced curtains, colourful shutters and window boxes overflowing with flowering plants. The rustic clay tiles glow in the late afternoon sunshine, adding a richness and warmth to this welcoming town.

St Jean Pied de Port (the foot of the pass) was the capital of the region of Basse-Navarre. It was fortified in the Middle Ages after the original site was razed by Richard the Lion-Heart in 1117. The Kings of Navarre, who rebuilt the town, continued to build the medieval loopholed walls, especially to protect the Citadel, which was built in 1628. The town walls run up the hill to join the corners of the Citadel, allowing for communication between the two during a siege.

It is a joy to explore the historic old upper town of St Jean and its environs. There is a particularly peaceful and beautiful circular route that begins near the Porte St Jacques. From here a steep path heads up to the Citadel, from which there are wide views down onto the town and out over the Pyrenees and into Spain. The path wanders through gateways and around the base of the Citadel's towering stone walls to its eastern side, then descends many steps to the River Nive near the Porte Nôtre Dame.

    The path continues away from town, following the river under cool leafy trees, and crossing over the Roman Pont Eyeraberri, returning back through the Rue D'Espagne and along to the Porte Nôtre Dame.

The Pilgrims' Office in St Jean Pied de Port

A Credencial del Peregrino (Pilgrim's Passport) is a very important document, as it allows you overnight accommodation in *albergues* (in Spanish or *auberge* in French) — pilgrims' refuges or hostels — as well as providing proof that you have walked the minimum 100 km to receive your Compostela Certificate from the Pilgrims' Office in Santiago.

You can register, then obtain your Passport and collect your scallop shell at the Pilgrims' Office in St Jean Pied de Port located near the Porte St Jacques. Payment is by donation.

The office is staffed by very friendly volunteers who will also advise you on *albergue* accommodation, the weather conditions over the Col de Lepoeder into Roncesvalles in Spain, and may be able to assist with many other details of the walk.

The Passport is marked with an official stamp at each night's accommodation along the Way. Further stamps can be obtained from churches, monasteries and restaurants. It becomes a very treasured possession, especially after the first stamp is received, symbolising the beginning of your journey to Santiago.

After registering at the Pilgrim's Office and collecting our Camino passport and shell, to our delight we discover a donkey grazing in the paddock next door. Two exceptionally charming young men were organising crates and boxes of photographic equipment for the donkey to carry. Australian freelance photographers, they were embarking the next day on a trip across Spain on the northern Atlantic route, before returning along the Camino de Santiago against the tide of pilgrims to record their experiences.

They had bought the donkey especially for their journey, just as Robert Louis Stevenson had purchased his donkey Modestine for his walk from Le Puy en Velay in 1878. We wonder whether their story would be like Stevenson's 'Travels with a Donkey' and if, like Stevenson, they would grow to admire their initially determined and disagreeable beast. Would the donkey become the centre of their travels?

The front page of our Passport and some stamps we collected at various *albergues* and monasteries along the Way.

THE SCALLOP SHELL AND WAYMARKERS

Today's pilgrims collect a scallop shell, the sign of the Camino, at the beginning of their journey, and wear it with pride along the Way.

The scallop shell was originally given to pilgrims when they reached Santiago and was sewn onto their clothes or hung from their staves as visible evidence that they had completed the walk and reached the final burial place of St James.

Traditionally, wearing the shell goes back to early Roman and pagan times, when the shells were found along the coast near Finisterre, 87 km west of Santiago. Serving as a talisman against evil, the shell was a symbol of fertility, rebirth and rejuvenation.

It appears on images of the pilgrim St James, on sculptures, prints, paintings, façades, altarpieces and coats of arms, and is incorporated into the architecture of Santiago Cathedral.

Despite having owned and operated an international trekking company for many years we had never identified ourselves with a trek symbol. For some, including me, it was difficult in the beginning to display the shell to other eyes. There can be a reserve, a sort of shyness, in openly declaring that you are on a pilgrimage.

However, the history of the walk, the timeless landscapes, the age-old places we visited, and the millions of Camino footsteps preceding us eventually pervaded our senses. The shell became part of us and engendered an unspoken bond with other walkers.

Within a very short time my shell was proudly attached to my backpack, and today one of our shells hangs welcomingly beside our front door.

Pilgrims are guided along the Way by regular, well-positioned, bright-yellow arrows and emblems of shells. Additionally, cement waymarkers indicate the distance to Santiago.

Waymarkers regularly appear along the Camino.

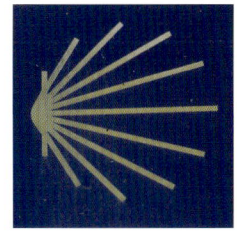 

TO ORISSON

We begin our journey, nervous yet excited.

We have mixed feelings on beginning the walk. The long build-up, the reading, the preparation, the travelling, the stories … they all contribute to an inner anxiety, a combination of excitement and nervousness. This will be a journey through an unknown land, which will challenge us physically and mentally. We are aware of the sacredness of the walk. Our senses are heightened. We anticipate a powerful inner journey, an acutely personal journey, and so we commence slowly and quietly, savouring every step on this spiritual path, past Nôtre Dame du Bout du Pont and under her protective arch where St Jean de Baptiste, with staff raised, farewells all pilgrims.

Beautiful scenery envelops us. David, a fellow walker, offers us local apples for afternoon tea. We head to a newly built private *auberge* at Orisson for our first night. Only 12 km out, it is a steep climb providing a good warm-up and time to break in our packs, each feeling heavy at 9 kg. We are passed by fellow pilgrims, some walking alone, others in twos and threes, or like David, who is walking with his dog Panda.

We are so pleased to reach the *auberge*. With only 18 beds available, there is a need to book ahead.

At an altitude of just under 1000 m, our auberge in Orisson has a deck overlooking the valleys and hills of the Pyrenees. It's a lovely place to sit, write and muse over the day's walk with other pilgrims. That evening we sit at a long table, enjoy wonderful food and wine and think of tomorrow's challenge over the pass into Spain.

We are billeted with four others, including a honeymooning French Canadian couple, and discover the challenges of shared accommodation. The husband snores so loudly he seems to rattle the bunks and shake the rafters. Unlike us his wife, who wore double earplugs, manages to get some sleep. We wonder if true love would survive and make a mental note to pack earplugs before we plan any further dormitory stays.

TO BURGUETE

The next morning, heading up the Route de Napoleon (Napoleon's Way) we look back on our safe refuge and watch the procession of black-faced sheep and cream-coloured cattle following us. They have a slow, purposeful walk, and seem in tune with the melodious soothing sound of the bells tied on wide leather collars around the necks of the lead animals.

At the end of the Peninsular War (1808–14) that pitted France against Spain, Portugal and Britain, Napoleon was driven over the Pyrenees by the Duke of Wellington. The route taken by his defeated armies from Roncesvalles to St Jean Pied de Port is known as the Route de Napoleon, and we are retracing this high mountain path as we cross the Pyrenees through the Col de Lepoeder.

TO BURGUETE

The Route de Napoleon with its spectacular views is very strenuous as it climbs up to the high plateau. The weather can also be extremely unpredictable as the Pilgrim Office in St Jean warned us. While it was raining lightly as we left Orisson, we did not expect the strength of the winds, which blew straight into us as we approached the highest pass, Col de Lepoeder (1450 m). To stand upright was an effort and places to shelter were few.

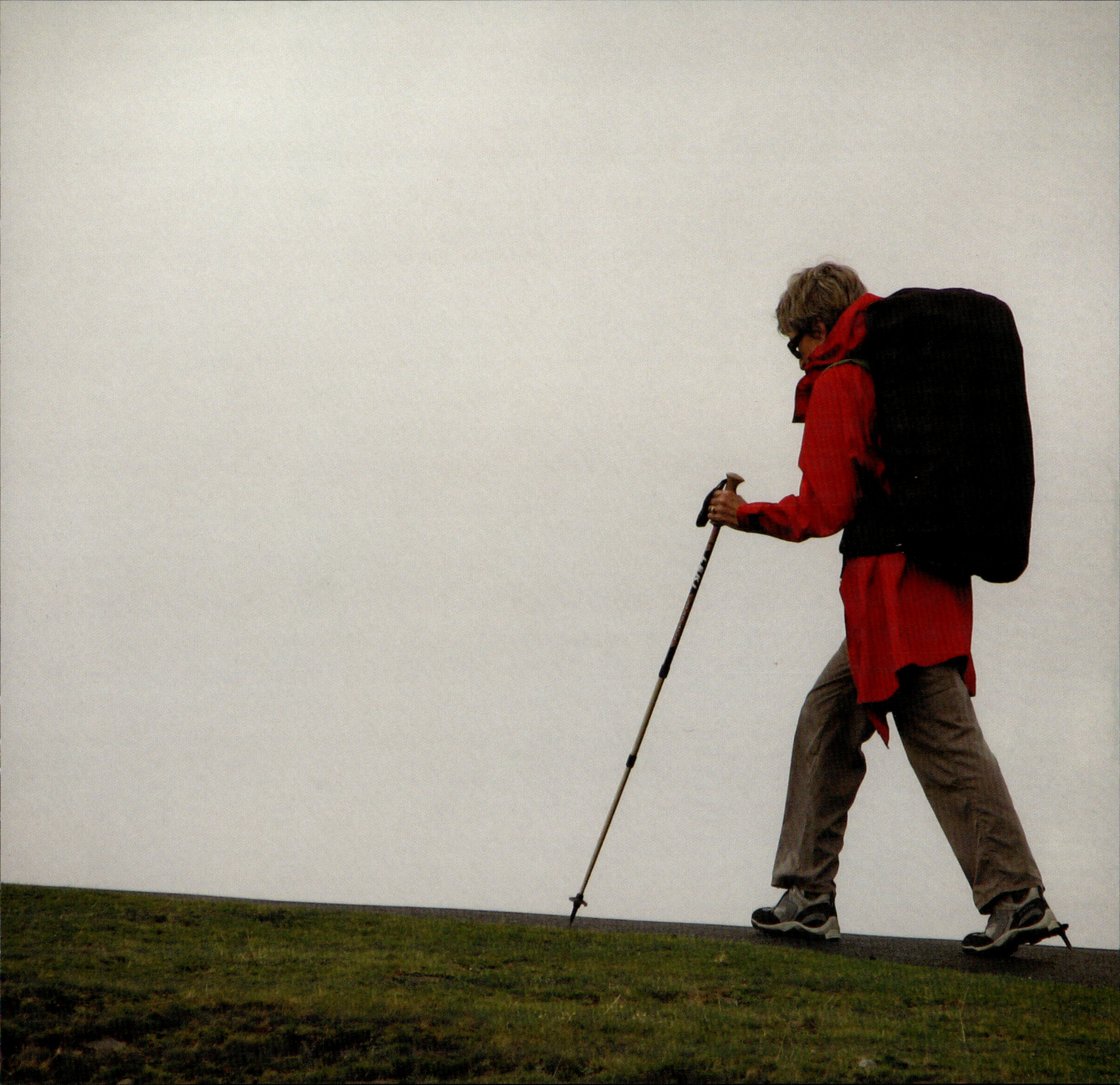

Handmade crosses placed at the feet of the statue.

At 1060 m the statue of the Virgin of Biakorri (also known as the Vierge d'Orisson) on the remote Pic d'Orisson urged us on and gave us comfort as the wind increased and the sky became greyer.

The small handmade crosses placed at her feet were symbols of reflection and dedication from those who had shared this magical place.

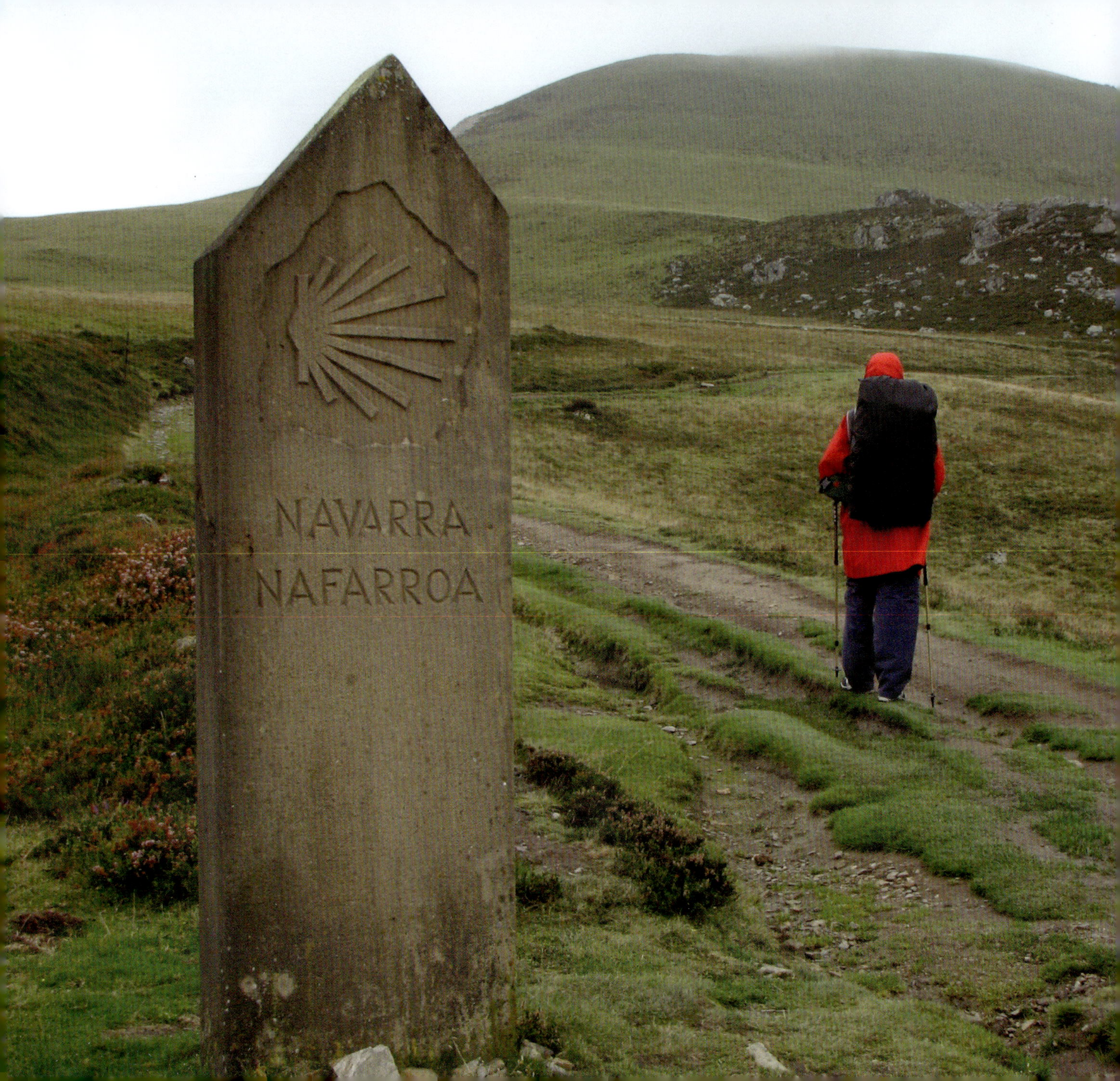
NAVARRA
NAFARROA

Leaving the hill road at the wayside cross, a natural path leads up through a gap in the ridge, past an emergency stone hut shelter and over the Spanish border. We approach the second highest point on the Way, the Col de Lepoeder, and before us are wide views west into Spain.

During the steep climb up to the pass we are at the mercy of the weather, with the fierce wind before us making our progress difficult. It seems the wind is determined to keep us out of Spain. As we cross the Pyrenees it is blowing at us from the west, pushing and shoving, snatching away backpack covers and ripping ponchos from the backs of their unfortunate owners. Leaning into the fierce blast, one young girl even has a contact lens torn from her eye.

Unsettled by the wind and in an effort to find shelter, the strong and woolly hill ponies run free.

Descending on the other side of the col the winds ease and the path becomes more protected by the thickening forests.

Autumn leaves dance in circles before us as they are stirred by flurries of wind. Settled leaves over the path provide a welcoming carpet of safety from the sticky mud.

Here the summer crocuses are growing in clumps under the protection of shady trees with their bright yellow stamens and their lavender petals reaching upwards. There are mushrooms too — flat, pointed, small, large, white, orange, spotted — prized by the locals and featuring in many traditional dishes.

A steep descent through a magnificent beech forest, one of the largest remaining forests of its kind in Europe, leads us to Roncesvalles, an entry point for Spanish pilgrims walking the Way of St James. It is a small complex of medieval buildings that have grown up around an ancient monastery. One of these buildings, originally a medieval pilgrim hospital, is a large *albergue* with over 120 beds in one dormitory!

With aching legs we head to the hotel next door to enjoy a welcoming beer and talk over our day's experiences with other pilgrims, sharing an easy spirit of solidarity. We meet a retired Dutch airline pilot and his wife and are amazed to discover that they spent two months walking from Holland, with the Camino de Santiago still ahead of them.

We are also greeted by our four-legged friend Panda — cheerful with his loving eyes set in their black panda circles. In the days to come we often thought of Panda's journey and wondered how he fared in Spain, where he would be sharing his nights in a tent with his master.

Past the former pilgrim hospital we head to our welcoming hotel at Roncesvalles.

TO BURGUETE

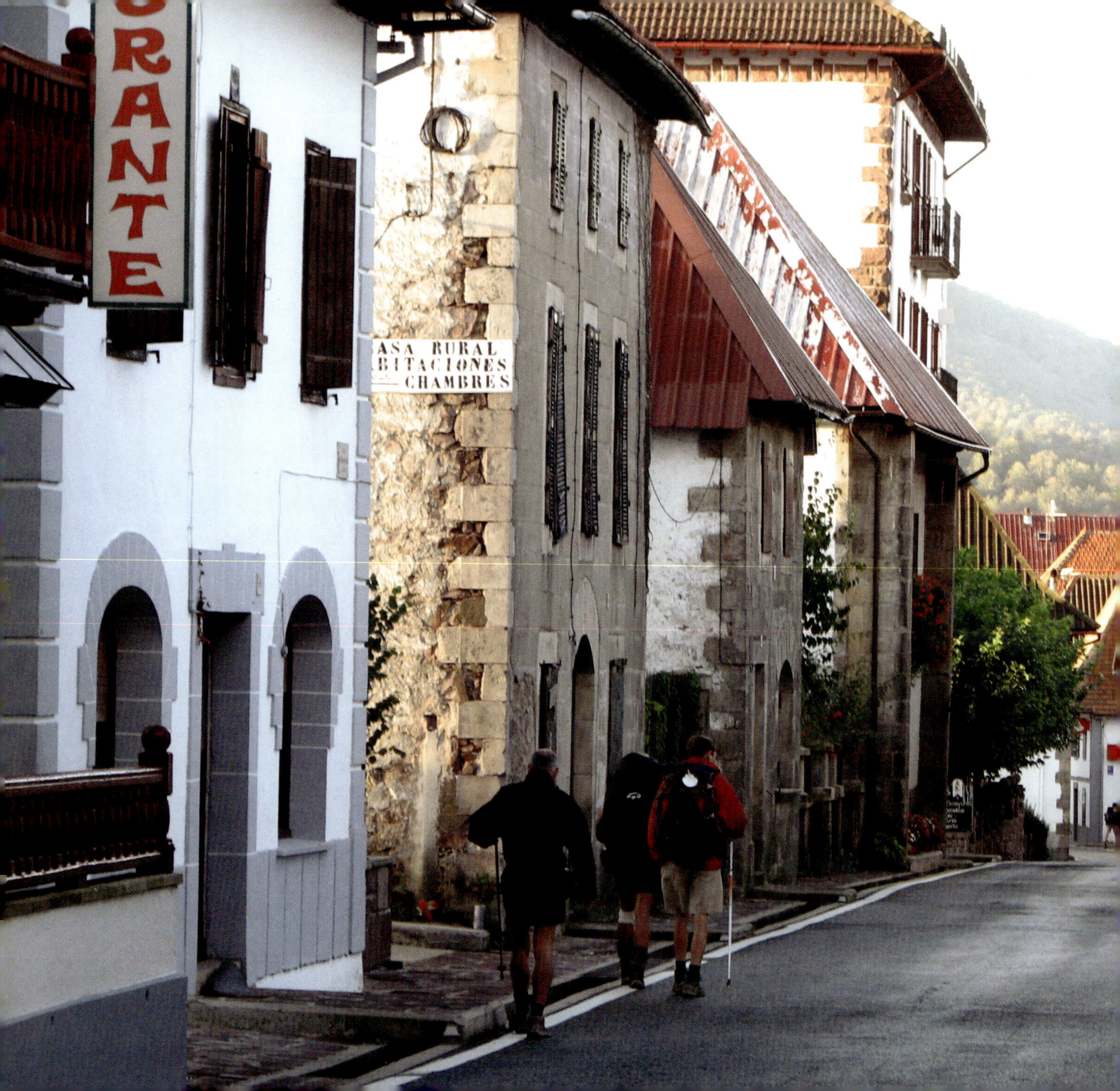

RANTE
ASA RURAL
BITACIONES
CHAMBRES

We walk a further 3 km from Roncesvalles to Burguete, a pristine, pretty village that was a favourite getaway for Ernest Hemingway. There are lots of pots dripping with flowers on the windowsills and verandahs. For our first night in Spain we took shelter in a charming Burguete hotel where Hemingway had actually stayed. The piano he played was still tantalizingly there, and he watched our arrival from photographs scattered around the walls.

To our delight we meet up with three Australian priests who had shared our table at Orisson, and join them for a jovial dinner at a nearby restaurant. After a magnificent paella washed down with fruity local wines, and warmed by several glasses of fine cognac, we hardly notice the light rain as we meander back along the cobbled street to our hotel.

From our room we can hear the familiar jingling sound of cow and sheep bells quieten into silence as the animals settle for the night. This harmony and peace envelops us as we too relax and look forward to another day of our journey.

Next morning one of the priests, who had been working as a missionary in Peru and spoke fluent Spanish, booked all our accommodation for the next stage. It was the first of many kindnesses we experienced along the way.

The colours of the old stone buildings in Burguete are pale and soft. The recent rain has filled the open street gutters with crystal-clear running water. We leave in the early morning. The high mountains of the Pyrenees are behind us as we walk through woodlands backlit by the sun, past fat, contented cattle, through old villages, crisscrossing rivers and up valleys.

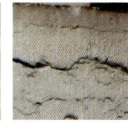

The colours of Navarre — the pinks, greys, the soft ochres, pale oranges and reds; the earthiness from the stone of the buildings; the terracotta of the roof tiles, the paths, the roads, the walls; so many pieces of history placed together, moulding and creating a peaceful scene, one into which the pilgrim becomes immersed.

TO ZUBIRI

Before making our steep descent to Zubiri, we walk down a path lined with interesting old stone fences made out of flat pieces of grey shale or slate placed intricately one on top of the other. The path places us beside a broken building filled with slushy cow dung and walks us tightly along its entire length. Looking through its open windows and doors and the jagged cracks of collapsed walls we are drawn into its interior. No plaque marks this site — no inscription informs us of its past. It is the ancient former pilgrim inn of Venta del Puerto, warm and peaceful in the late afternoon sun.

Our guide book describes it as a ruin and a cattle shelter. Other books do not mention it at all. With its roof and floors collapsing, its outer walls leaning, its windows open and unprotected — to us this is an especially powerful place. We feel a presence from the building's life before cattle, so many centuries ago. We are moved by the power of the site to evoke a deep feeling for its ancient and spiritual past, and think of the wondrous skills of those who built this simple yet commanding structure so long ago and of the thousands who have taken refuge here on their way to and from Santiago.

The now derelict ancient former pilgrim inn of Venta del Puerto.

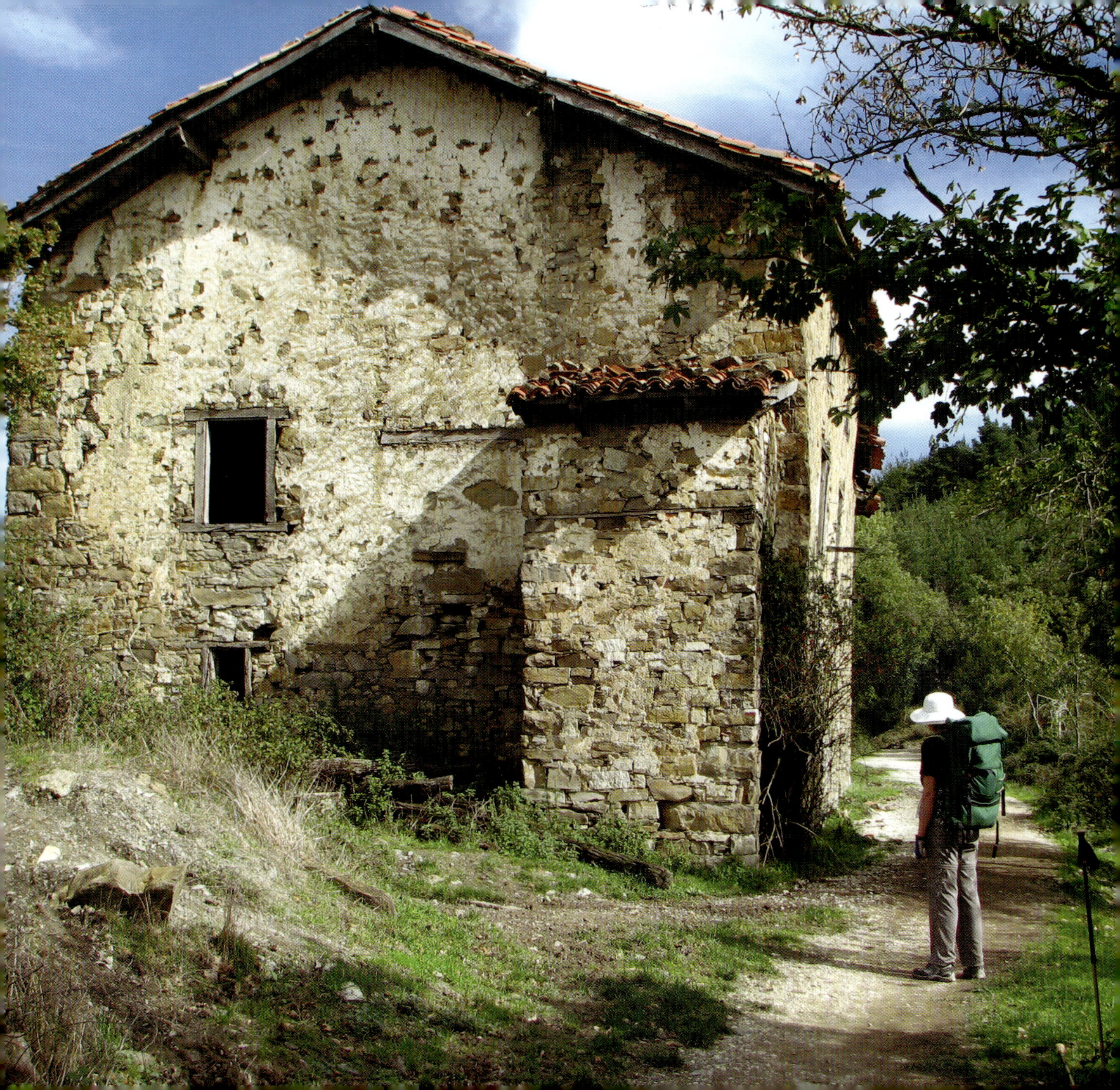

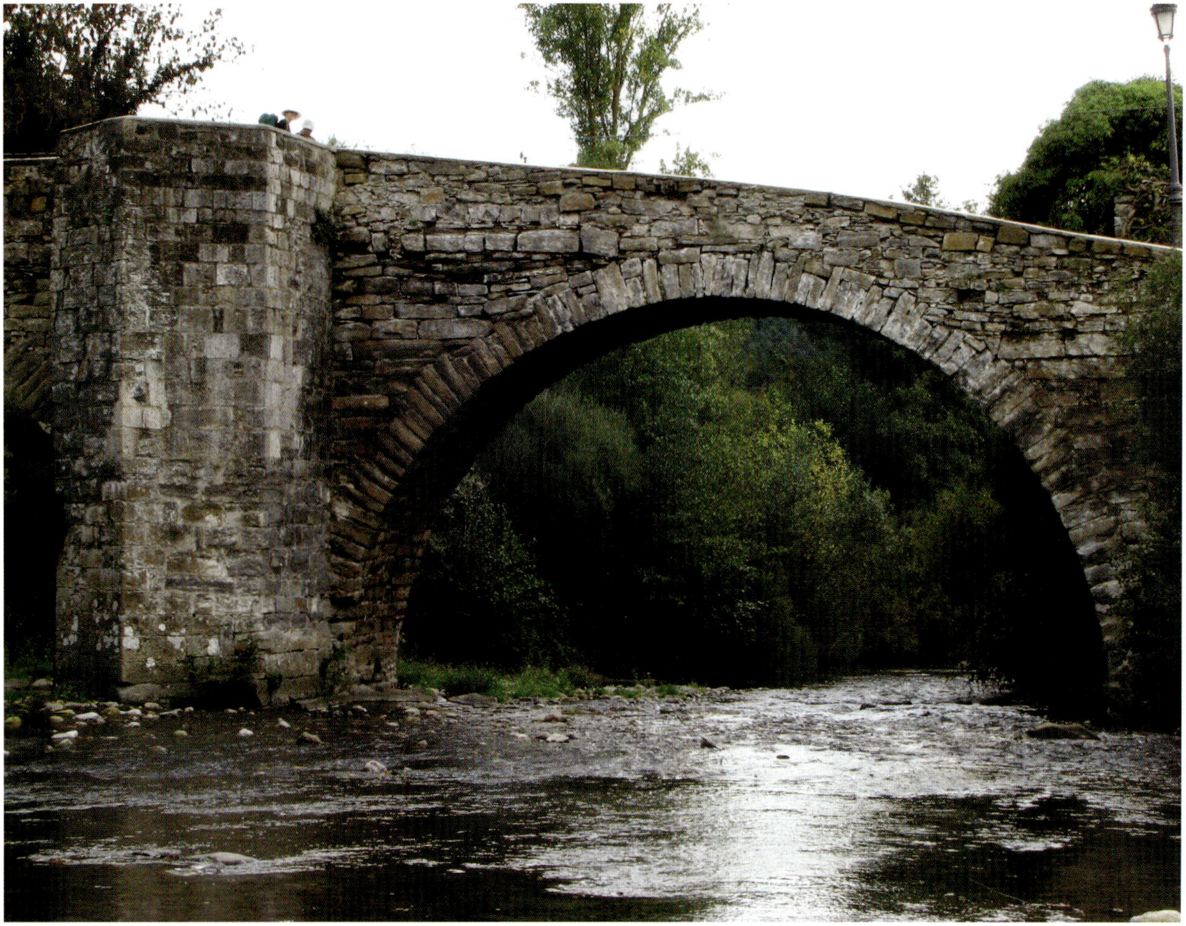

History records that in 778 Charlemagne's rearguard army, led by Roland, was defeated in this region. Despite fighting the Spanish successfully in Zaragoza and Pamplona, Roland's stepfather, Ganelon, allied himself with the King of Zaragoza against Charlemagne. On being attacked, Roland desperately tried to call Charlemagne by blowing the oliphant, a horn supposedly made from a unicorn's horn, sending out a supernatural melancholic wail. Ganelon, however, persuaded Charlemagne not to leave the Pyrenees immediately, and by the time Charlemagne returned, Roland had been killed. Charlemagne pursued and annihilated the enemy's armies and executed Ganelon in France. Even though Roland was buried in Roncesvalles, it is said that some pilgrims can feel the sadness of Roland and hear the wail from the horn as they walk along this part of the route.

We share our path with marathon runners today, as we descend carefully down a very slippery, steep and muddy section. They pass us at breakneck speed, noisy and impatient, determined to complete their 22 km in the fastest time. Men and women, young and not so young, dressed in tightly fitting, brightly coloured lycra — like a swarm of bees they charge by, splashing us with mud.

Tired, we reach Zubiri, crossing the Rio Arga over the medieval double-arched Puente de Rabia (the Bridge of Rabies), and walking past the old hospital that was built to house lepers. The Puente de Rabia was so called because it was believed that cattle crossing under it would be cured of rabies if they turned in a circle three times.

Zubiri is a small industrial town with a busy highway as its main street. It was lacking facilities, however we are able to book into a very comfortable pension near the bridge.

TO PAMPLONA

The Camino leads us into the old city of Pamplona over a drawbridge and through the Portal de Francia. It is a beautiful, elegant, vibrant university town and the centre of rich Basque history with a plethora of fine buildings, museums and art galleries.

Destroyed and rebuilt many times, Pamplona had a succession of ruling cultures until the 8th century, when it became an independent power and the capital of what was later the Kingdom of Navarre.

The narrow, winding medieval streets are rich in colour, crisscrossing through the old quarter of this gracious old city.

We head for the main square, the Plaza del Castillo, where the cafés are inviting and the shops tempting. As in all Spanish towns, *plazas* are meeting places, especially at lunchtime and at the end of the day when they fill with people. The young and old promenade, children play, music can be heard and spare tables are few. A lively atmosphere continues until late into the night.

We meet familiar faces and enjoy friendships created by the Camino's spirit of camaraderie: friendships that may not be long lasting, but are very special during the journey.

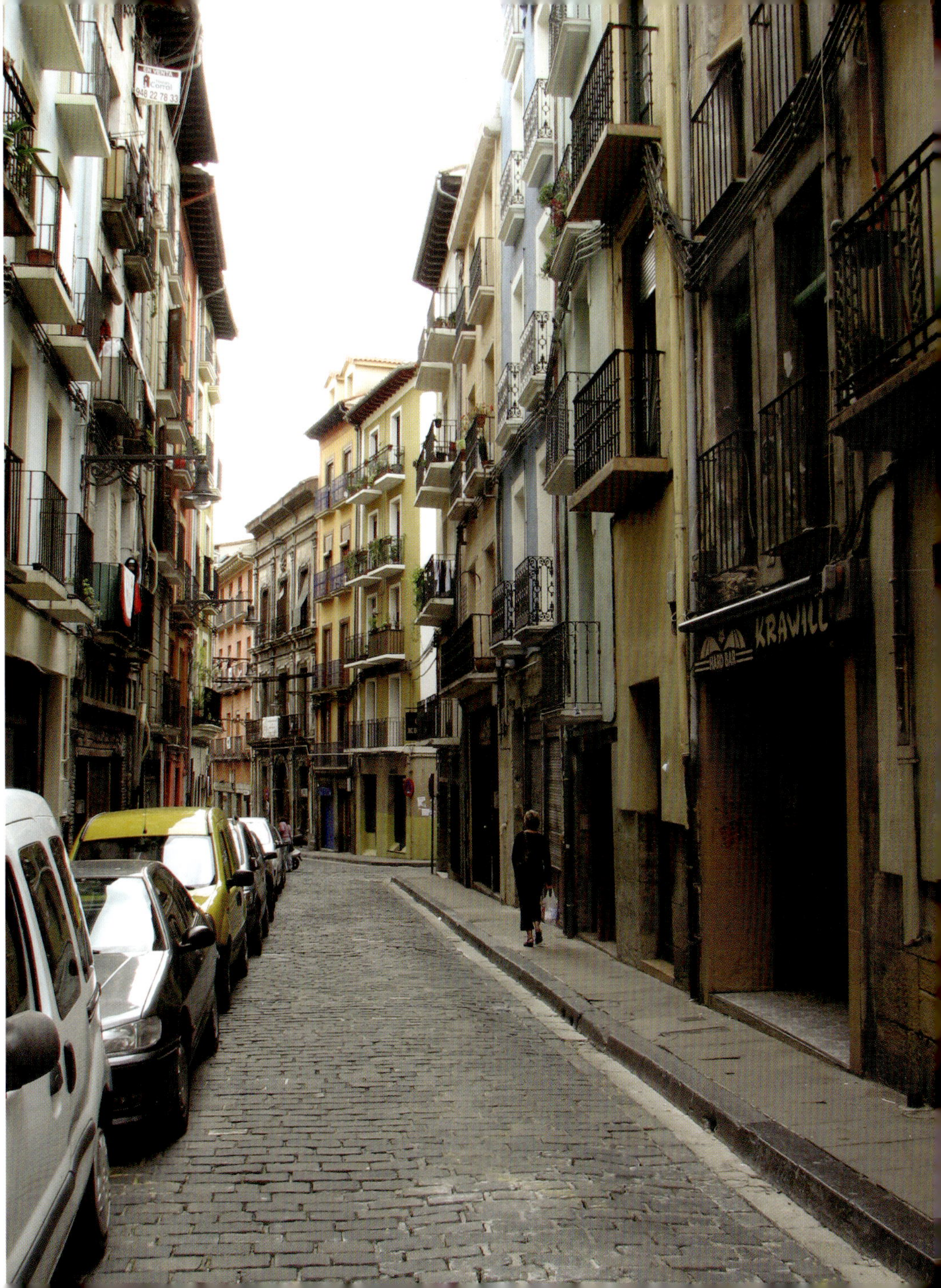
Corral
948 22 78 33
KRAWILL

Pamplona Cathedral is an austere Gothic structure which houses the alabaster mausoleum of King Carlos III and his wife, Doña Leonor. The cloisters are beautiful, with delicate French plateresque façade. A museum houses wondrous religious art and fine woodcarvings of the Virgin Mary dating from the 12th to the 14th century.

Every July Pamplona explodes in gaiety and fun, and is wild and noisy with dance and fireworks as it holds the San Fermin Festival, which lasts for one week. The bulls run through the old city to the Plaza de Toros, past a large statue of Ernest Hemingway who wrote about the event in his book *Death in the Afternoon*.

We have enough time to explore and enjoy the many treasures of Pamplona — old wooden doors, peppers hanging in the windows and intricate designs in the ancient pebbled pavements.

TO PUENTE LA REINA

After the bustle and noise of Pamplona and a tiring walk over the hills of Pardon, it is a pleasure to stop for a coffee at a newly built *albergue* in Uterga — an 18-bed private hostel.

The countryside is changing. It is more open and drier, with fewer trees. The colours are richer and deeper, and there is fragrance in the air from spent sunflowers, maize and grape vines.

We are soothed by the tranquillity of the ploughed fields as we walk towards a low range of hills and ancient villages.

Between Uterga and Óbanos a short circular detour leads through open dry farmland to the beautiful Gothic church of Santa Maria de Eunate. Situated alone on a slight rise, the building glows in the sunlight. This tiny church was built to provide a cemetery for pilgrims who died while making their journey.

Octagonal in shape, it is surrounded by a freestanding cloister of delicate double pillars. There are two entrance doors, each decorated with plant and animal reliefs. At one end there is a pentagonal apse, and sitting atop a slate roof are two large church bells within a triangular tower.

We are moved by the greeting stapled to the ancient entrance which welcomes visitors to this 'tranquil and holy place; a silent place which allows time for reflection; a loving house where no-one is a foreigner'. Inside, the diffused light from the high opaque windows drifts slowly down like chalk dust, settling upon the soft greys and pinks of the old stone floor and walls.

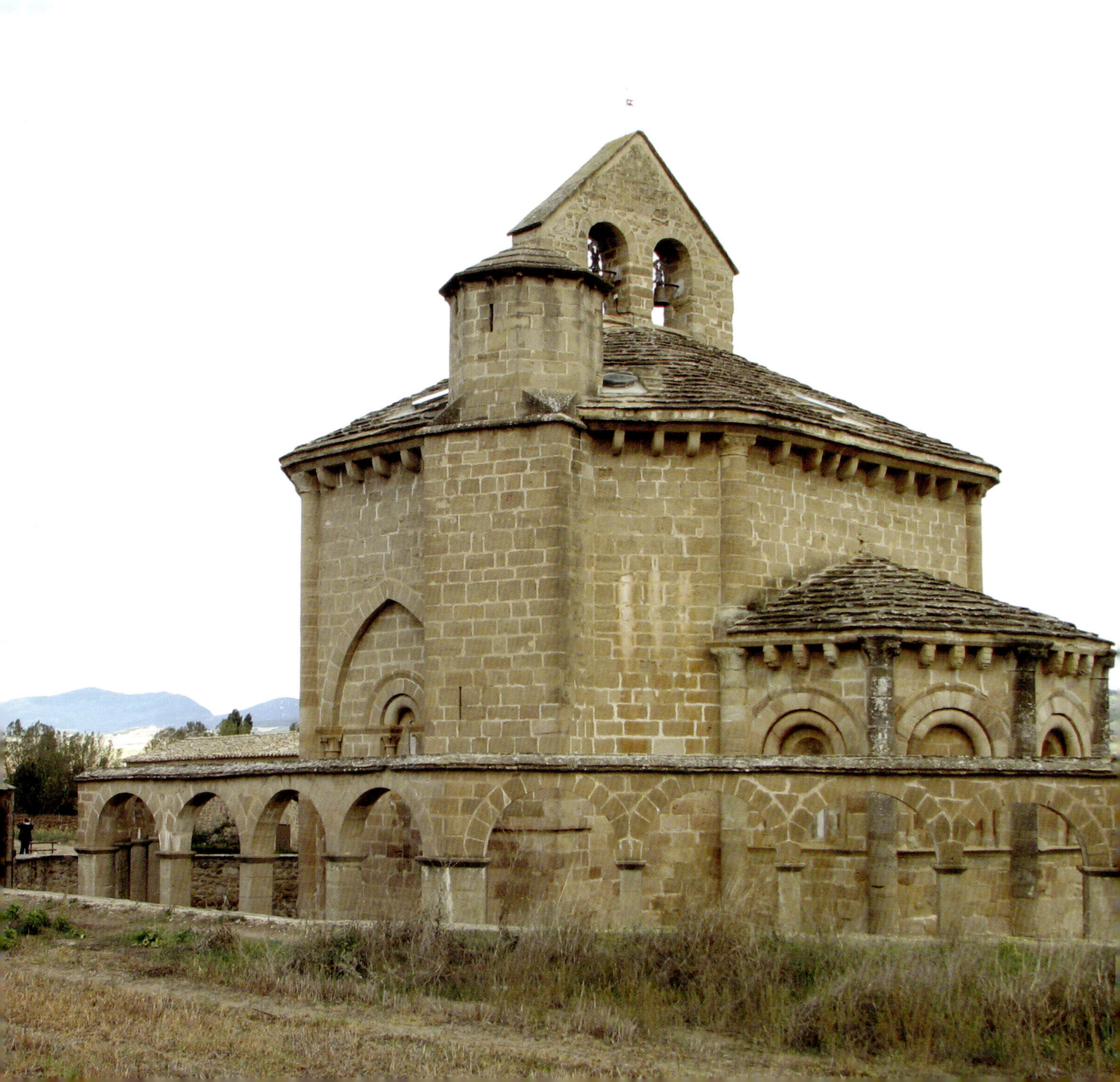

In the apse of this simply decorated church an ancient wooden statue of Mary and Child sits upon a stone plinth. It is powerfully captivating. Shining in her gold cloak and crown, Mary has a presence that makes you want to sit awhile in peace and contemplation. Her eyes draw you to her; they penetrate and follow your movements; her outstretched hand beckons and offers kindness and love.

The architecture of the Church of Santa Maria de Eunate has been linked with the Knights Templar, a military Christian order created in the aftermath of the First Crusade of 1096 to protect European pilgrims heading to the Holy Lands. The order was sanctioned by the Papacy in 1128, and over the next 200 years it created an innovative and effective infrastructure across Europe. Of particular interest were the order's financial techniques, which are considered the foundation of modern banking.

The knights grew in number, prosperity and power, and soon became the strongest fighting unit of the Crusades. However, their success in the Crusades did not last, and conflicts emerged between them and the royalty of France. Philip IV deeply resented being in debt to the order. He decided not only to renege on the debt, but also to seize the wealth and property of the order for himself. In the early 1300s he had the Pope disband the entire order and convict the Templars of heresy. Many were arrested, tortured and burnt at the stake. With the disappearance of the order, much of the infrastructure they had created came to an end.

However, their architecture, as seen in this small church, remained. In their brief period of power they constructed a great number of buildings, including many castles and citadels, built for defence. Being practical and strong, some of these buildings are still in use today.

This church is an example of the Templars' distinctive design and craftsmanship in that it is octagonal, with a semicircular internal apse and vaulted openings rather than arches (except for its outer porch). It is functional and simple, not elaborate or ornate, giving it a powerful, protective presence. It is a sanctuary for peace and spirituality — one of the jewels on the Camino.

The impact of the Eunate Church remained with us as we walked on through fields of dried sunflowers and farmland to Óbanos, a delightful village built on a slight rise, with streets of buildings resplendent with armorial crests and full of flowering pot plants on windowsills and in balconies.

Apparently Duke William X of Aquitaine (St William, or Guillén, or Guilhem), killed his sister, Felicia, in Óbanos because she had refused to return to her duties at the Court of Aquitaine after a pilgrimage to Santiago. Suffering remorse, William also made a pilgrimage to Santiago and upon returning relinquished his nobility and wealth to live as a hermit in the nearby mountain hermitage of Arnotegui. The large and striking Gothic Church of San Juan Bautista (St John the Baptist) in Óbanos contains the skull of St William, the cranium covered in silver.

Every year in September the villagers make a festive pilgrimage to the hermitage. The statue of the Virgin of Arnotegui, along with a statue of St James, is in the Church of St John the Baptist in Óbanos, and it is here the play known as *The Mystery of Óbanos* is performed every two years.

Aquitaine was a new power that arose in France in the early 12th century and remained independent until the 13th century. This, too, was a period of awakening of a new era for Spain as the crusades inspired a rise in patriotism and religion. Aquitaine and other Christians took the opportunity to reconquer lost territories that resulted in the decline of Moorish culture in Spain and its withdrawal to the south.

A restaurant in the town serves us a wonderful lunch of local trout and an excellent dry white wine. As our lunch progresses

The church of St John the Baptist and quiet streets (below) in Óbanos.

we are joined by many men — farmers, villagers, old men, young men — but no women. There is great chatter, great faces, great enthusiasm and great eating.

Yet outside there is not a sign of activity; there are only quiet streets, shuttered windows and closed doors. Even the imposing Church of San Juan Bautista, with its dark and cool portico, is shut. Unable to enter we admired the modern metal statue of Jesus on the cross in the *plaza* outside and continued on to the next town, Puente la Reina (the Queen's bridge). This is where Charlemagne is reputed to have stayed after his victorious battle in Cizur against the Moors.

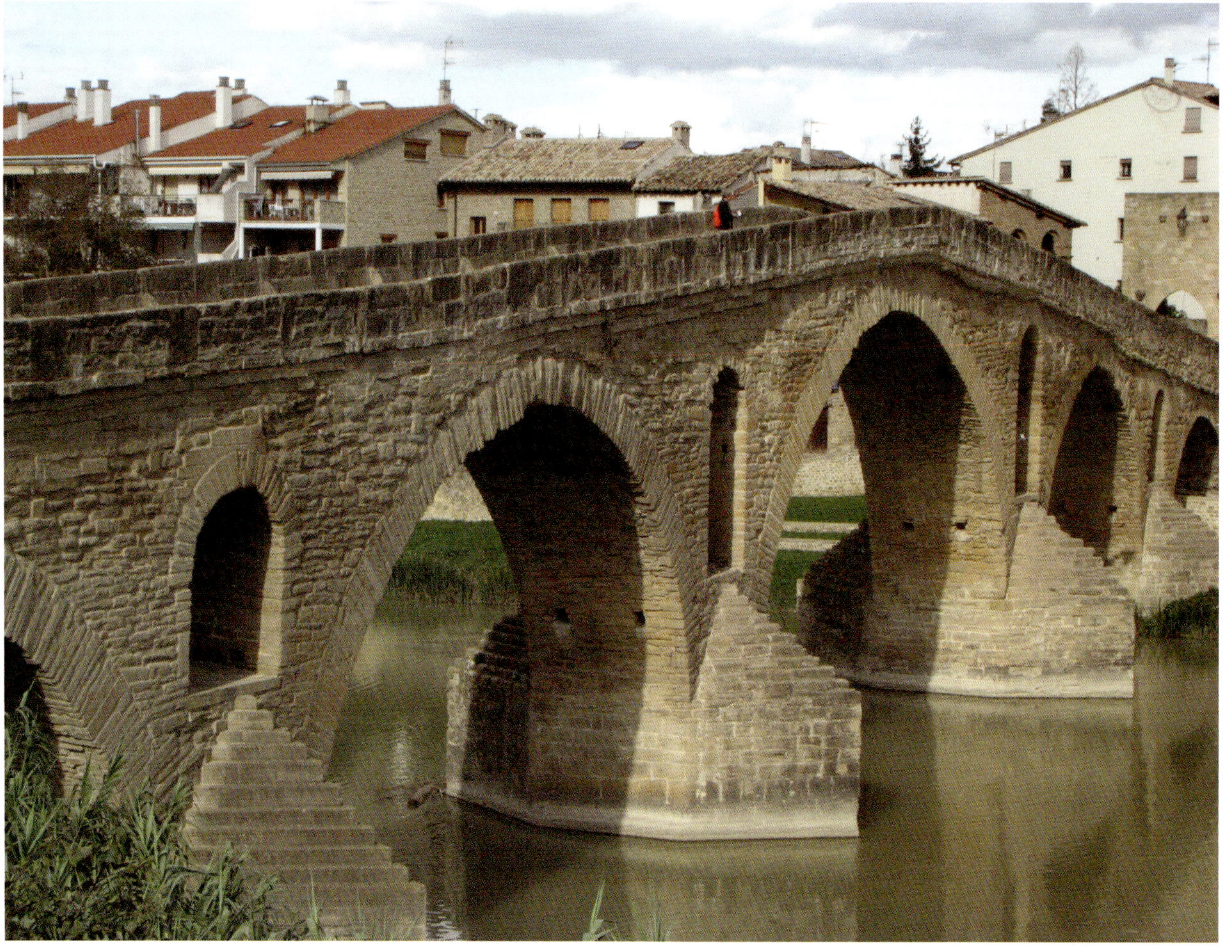

Since leaving Zubiri, the Camino has crossed the Rio Arga many times, and at Puente la Reina the river becomes a larger waterway. So large, in fact, that in the 11th century Queen Dona Major (Muniadona de Castille), wife of Sancho III, built a magnificent six-arch bridge to span the river so that pilgrims would no longer have to risk their lives crossing in deep water on their way to Santiago. The bridge and the town's main street are consequently named after her.

Legend has it that a *chori*, a little bird, would fly to a tower in the centre of the bridge containing a Renaissance carving of the Virgin Mary, and with its wings would clean away any cobwebs attached to the statue and with its moistened beak wash Mary's face. This was taken as an auspicious event and caused much celebration among the town's people. The *chori* came back every year until 1846, when the statue was extensively damaged and taken away. The bird was never seen again.

Puente la Reina is an important village on the Camino, as it is where the other pilgrimage route from France converges. It is also an interesting example of an ancient 'one street' village — its narrow, straight and elegant main street leading down to the Rio Arga has a strong medieval atmosphere, with Gothic architecture and many churches. It passes the imposing Iglesia de Santiago (Church of Santiago) with its dark interior lit by gilded pieces. The church's powerful exterior presence is enhanced by its tall square tower, in which birds' nests seem to compete for space with the church bells.

Close by is the Iglesia del Crucifijo (Church of the Crucifix), which was built by the Knights Templar. They established themselves in the village in 1142 and held it until their expulsion and dissolution in the early 14th century. Today the church houses a fine Gothic crucifix from Germany. Legend has it that upon arriving at Puente la Reina, en route to Santiago, the cross could not be carried any further.

This small church has a dark interior that is said to have great acoustics allowing a single voice to resonate like a choir as it travels to heaven and returns as the sound of angels. Such a poetic tale reminded us of the architect Gaudi's response to a question about why he had decorated the tall spires on the Temple Expiatori de la Sagrada Familia in Barcelona with such wonderful detail even though they were so high. He replied, 'because the angels will be able to enjoy them'.

We stay the night at a delightful hotel that was formerly an old manor house, beautifully restored and quite luxurious. One of the joys after walking all day is being able to soak in a warm bath, and our deep bath, with complimentary bath gel, is exceptionally relaxing and bubbly.

We are joined for dinner by a fellow pilgrim from Austria. His wife had recently died, and in trying to rid himself of his grief he was walking up to 40 km every day. Although we were not to meet up with him again, we often thought of him and hoped the spirit of the Camino would guide him.

TO ESTELLA

The Roman occupation of the Iberian Peninsula began around 200 BC and there is a section of very early Roman road near Cirauqui, between Puente la Reina and Estella.

A total of 85,300 km of roads were built throughout Europe and North Africa to support the Roman military campaign. They were magnificent engineering feats, essential to enable the Roman armies to move quickly and vital to commerce throughout the vast empire. The proverb that 'all roads lead to Rome' was very true.

To walk on such ancient history and to think about how these roads were constructed is very humbling. The skills of the engineers, stonemasons and labourers who constructed these roads were amazing.

There were detailed laws and regulations governing the construction of Roman roads. The 'Twelve Tables', dating back to 450 BC, specified that roads should be 2.48 m wide where straight and 4.96 m wide where curved, but in fact the roads were anything from 1.16 m to 7.44 m wide. Milestones were placed at every 1000 paces and way stations were established every 25–30 km. Further regulations controlled the use of chariots, coaches and commercial carts.

Also within this section of the Camino are two wonderful single-arch stone Roman bridges. Both are still in use, although one is in a dilapidated condition. Again we are overwhelmed by the power of these ancient structures and the skill it took to build them. We touch their stones and rest awhile to contemplate their history. To have the opportunity to walk on such beautiful monuments to a past civilisation is a credit to the Roman builders.

In complete contrast, we walk alongside a two-lane highway and under a modern aqueduct and wonder whether these will be standing in 2000 years!

TO ESTELLA

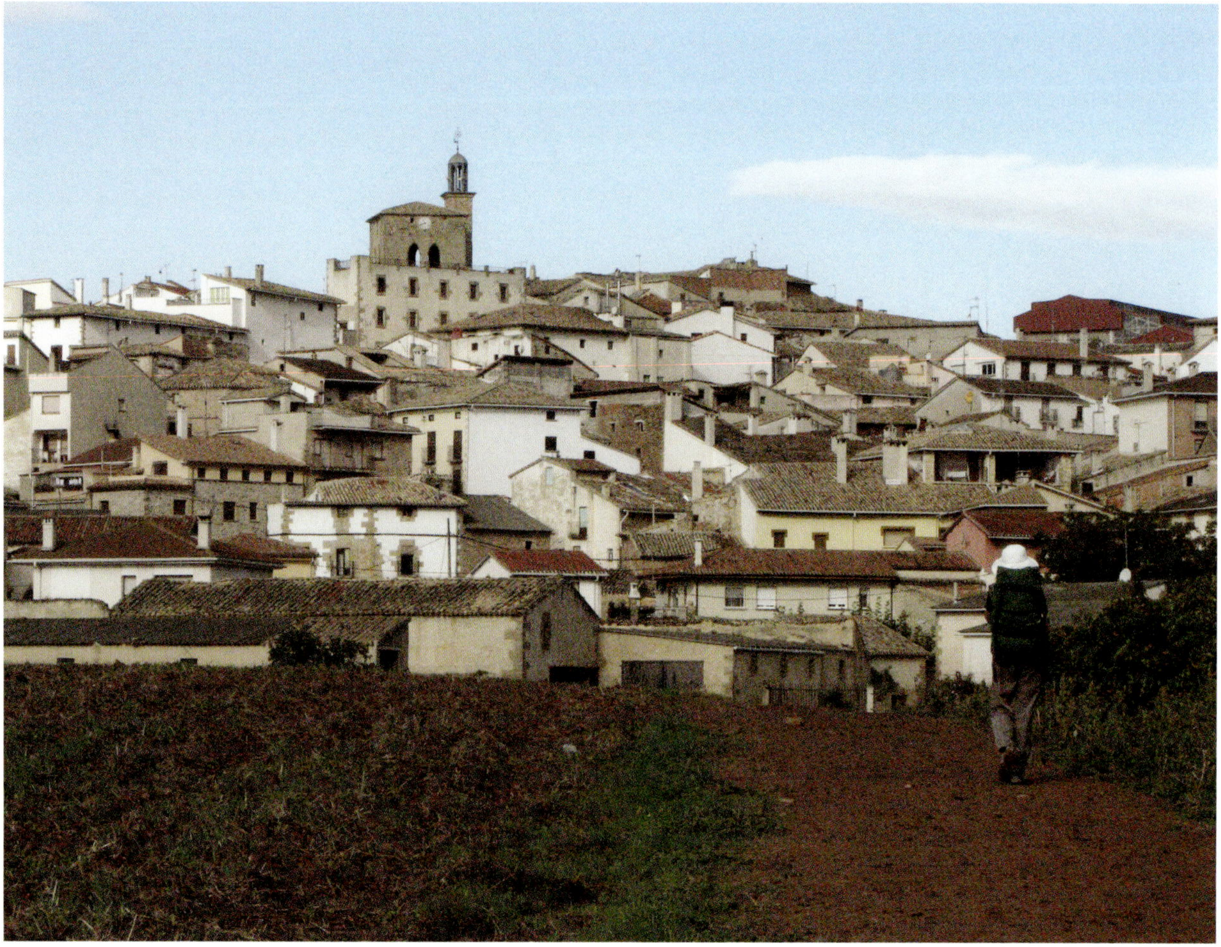

A reflective walk follows through open, gently rolling country past vineyards and olive trees to the medieval hilltop villages of Mañeru and Cirauqui, both dominated by their church spires.

Mañeru, with its links to the Knights Templar, is now a sleepy, peaceful village. Cirauqui can be seen in the distance. Its name is Basque meaning 'viper's nest', referring to the rocky hill on which it is built. It is an enchanting place, with narrow winding labyrinthine streets and ancient stone buildings, many with armorial crests, ornate balconies and shuttered doors.

We are nearing the end of our first week of walking. Our inner feelings of peace, of letting go, and being in the now have grown stronger as the timeless rhythm of the Camino envelops us.

> Yesterday is today's memory
> Tomorrow is today's dream
> Let us embrace the past with remembrance
> and the future with longing.
> Today is the now, the being.
>
> *Kahlil Gibran*

The Court of Justice in Estella.

Taking a right-hand turn off the Camino we enter Estella through the Plaza San Martin with its central fountain overlooked by the Court of Justice with its balcony adorned with flowering pots and colourful flags. Continuing across the Rio Ega we climb wonderful streets into the old quarter, admired for its historic buildings and plazas. There is so much to explore in this picturesque, compact town, built on the bend of a tree-lined river. The town's Basque name is Lizarra, which in Spanish is Estella ('star') — a Way of the Stars to Compostela.

Originally a primary reception point for the growing flood of pilgrims along the Camino, in the 11th century Estella became a prominent and prosperous town attracting many artisans and tradesmen who built a great number of its fine buildings. Disharmony and open fighting, however, developed between the various groups who settled here — the French, the Jews and the Navarrese. Despite the Kings of Navarre unifying their separate boroughs in 1266, fighting did not cease, finally resulting in the Jewish group being expelled in the 14th century.

Estella's unsettled times continued through the centuries — it was attacked by Napoleonic troops and involved in the War of Independence. In the 1800s further fighting took place in this area when the town became a stronghold of the Carlists during the conflict over the successor to King Ferdinand VII.

The fortified tower of the 13th century Iglesia de San Pedro de la Rúa (Church of San Pedro de la Rúa) sits high above the town at the top of steep steps leading up from the Court of Justice. The partially destroyed cloisters with their tranquil garden are especially beautiful.

Content to sit awhile, savour the gardens and explore the ruins in the late afternoon light, we become so absorbed in its peace and beauty that we lose track of time. When we finally regain our senses we find that the entrance doors of the church have been locked. Eventually, after much banging, an old man appears from within and comes to our rescue.

Opposite is the restored Palacio de los Reyes de Navarra (Palace of the Kings of Navarre), which is now a museum. Crossing the river and heading up to the main square, the Plaza de los Fueros, there is the imposing Iglesia de San Juan Bautista. The *plaza* is a vibrant square filled with cafés and people.

The 13th century Iglesia de San Pedro de la Rúa.

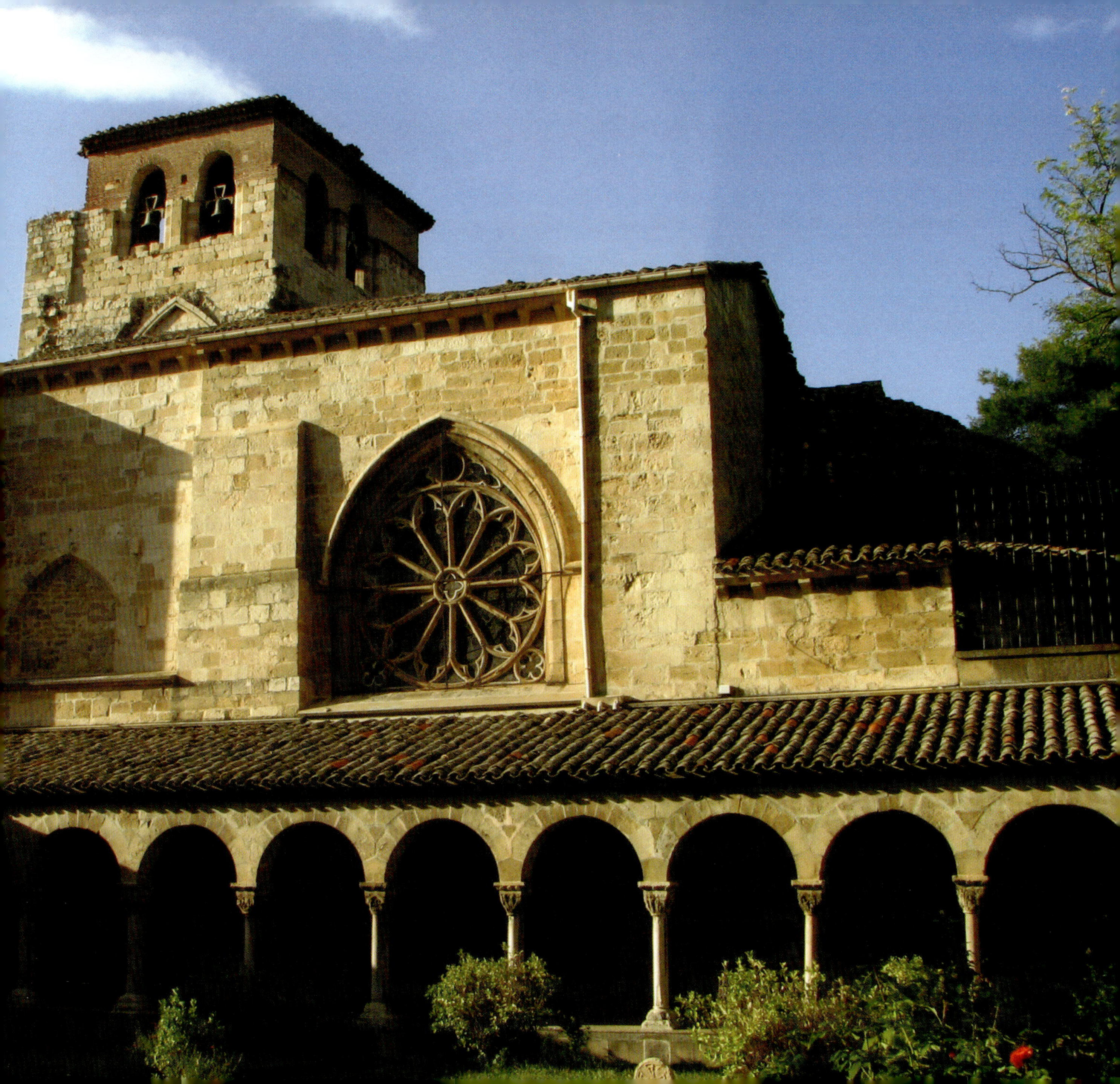

TO LOS ARCOS

The next morning we walk into the Bodegas Irache, the Irache Winery, which in 1991 installed a pilgrim fountain with two taps: one supplies water and the other a very acceptable red wine. The fountain was set in an enclosed courtyard with gates that are locked overnight. It was quite a busy gathering place for pilgrims and there was almost a party atmosphere with many photos taken of water being replaced by wine in everyone's drinking bottles!

Nearby the ancient Benedictine Monasterio de Irache, built on the lower slopes of the Montejurra mountain range, is glowing in the early morning light. Within the monastery complex there is a beautiful Romanesque door on the 12th century Iglesia de San Pedro, as well as a rather crumbling yet wondrous 16th century cloister.

The monastery has been associated with Roncesvalles and the Camino since the 10th century, and it is thought that some parts of the building could date back to the time of the Visigoths, who established themselves in the Iberian Peninsula in 495, following the end of the Roman Empire. They, in turn, were invaded by the Moors from North Africa in 717. The Moors controlled much of Spain until the Reconquista by Christian forces, which began later in the 8th century and culminated with the defeat of the last Muslim ruler of Granada in 1492.

Since 1985, due to the decreasing number of Benedictine monks living there, the monastery has been run by the government and now houses a museum.

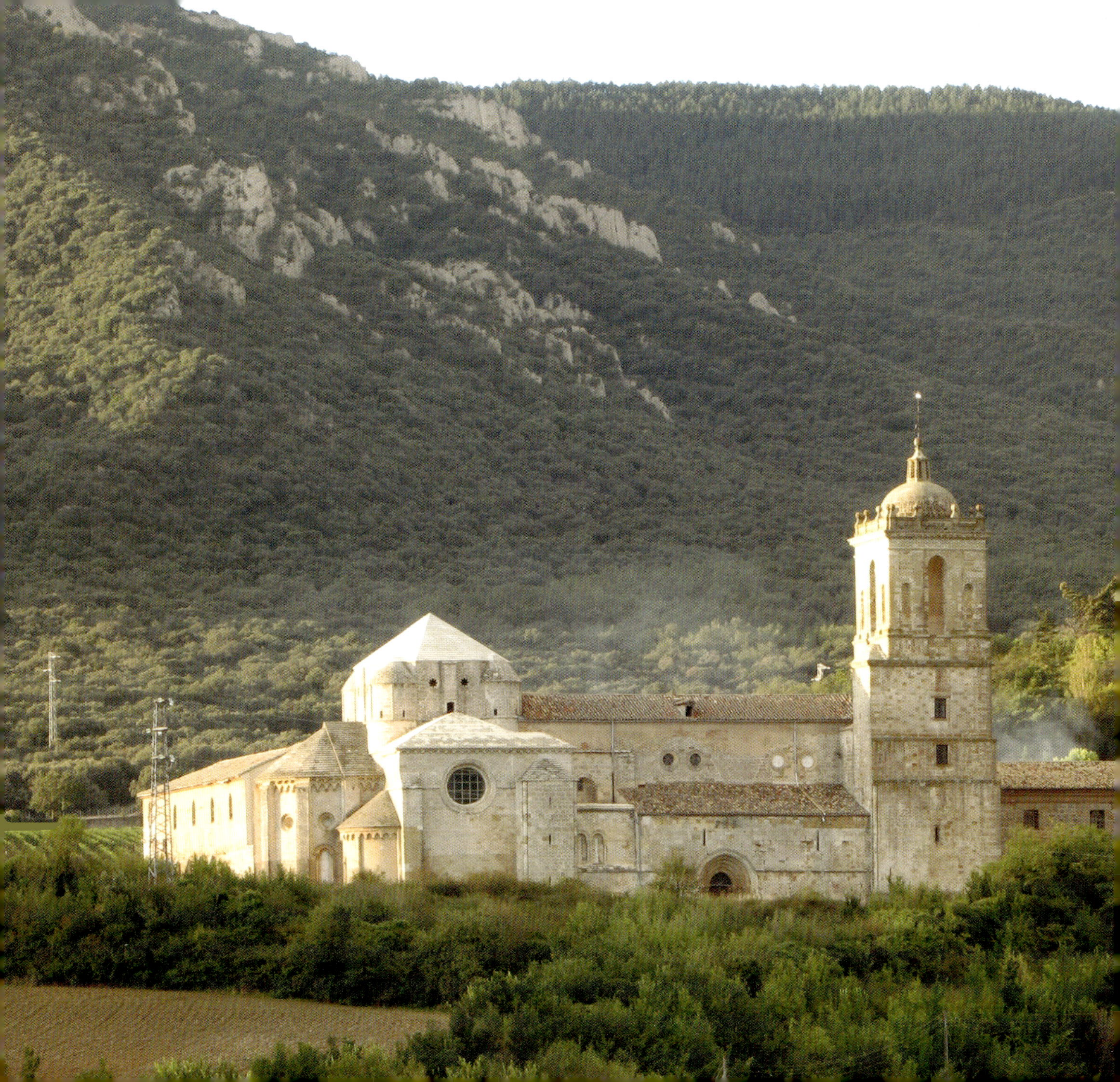

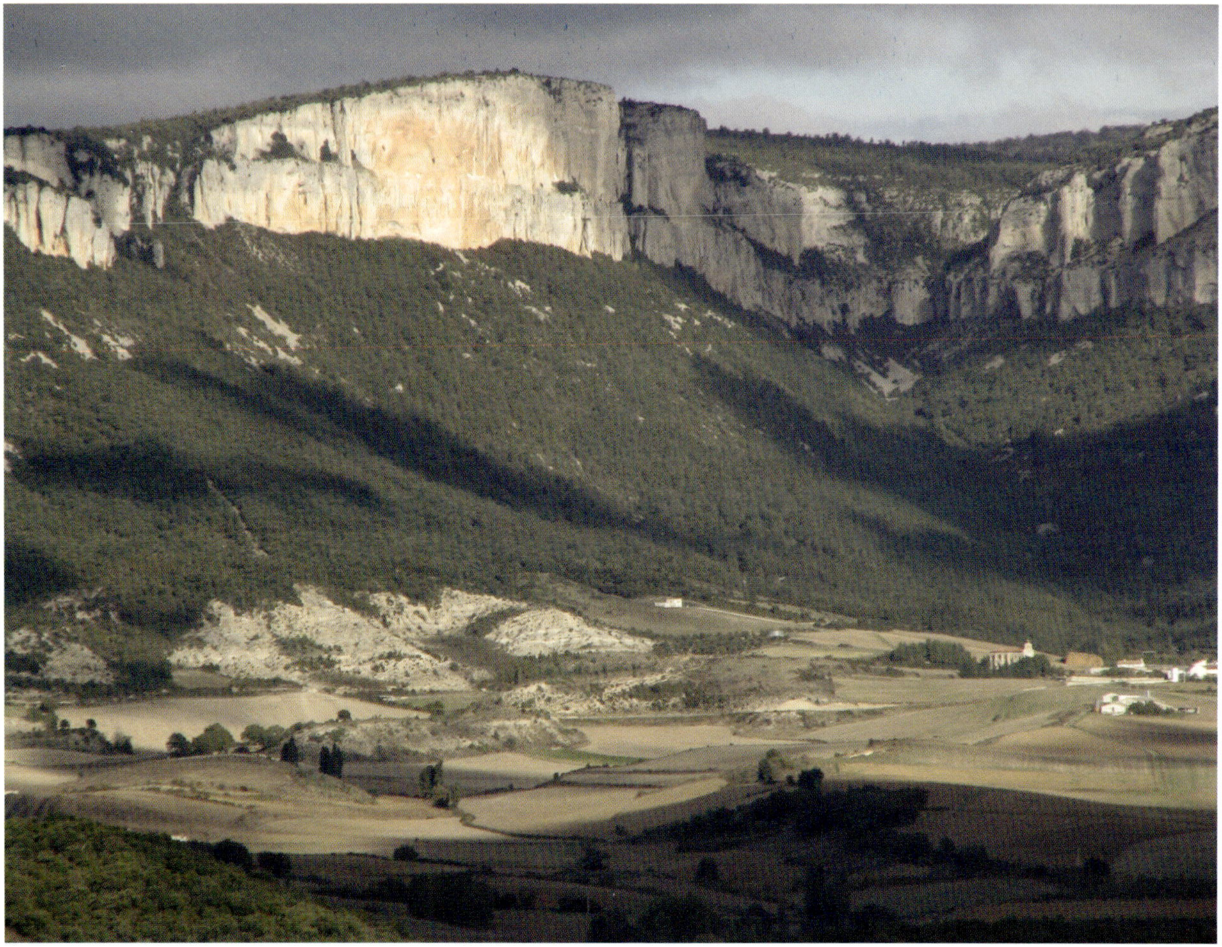

We are in Navarre, which is one of three territories inhabited by the Basque people and claimed by Basque nationalism. It is now an autonomous region within Spain, but was once an independent kingdom. The other two territories of the Basques are the Northern Basque Country (Pays Basque) in southwest France and the Basque Country (País Vasco or Euskadi), an autonomous community made up of three provinces and the only region currently recognised by the Spanish authorities as 'Basque'.

We have been walking through Basque territory since our departure from St Jean Pied de Port, the capital of Pays Basque. Navarre's capital is Pamplona, and tonight's destination, Los Arcos, will be our last night in the Basque Country before entering the territory of La Rioja.

Leaving Estella, we walk alongside the Montejurra mountain range, a rather formidable sight with its huge creamy rugged rock faces. It is an area with a tumultuous past: Basque warlords fought over this region through much of the Middle Ages, and in the 1800s the mountains and the surrounding villages and countryside became the stronghold of Carlists. Three Carlist wars ravaged the area, ending only when Carlos VII won back his Bourbon throne by force of arms.

The Carlists emerged when Ferdinand VII of Spain died in 1833 and installed his fourth wife as Queen Regent on behalf of their infant daughter Isabella II. This splintered the country into two factions, the Isabellinos and the Carlists. The Carlists supported the Bourbon dynasty and wanted the throne to pass to Ferdinand's brother, Carlos V.

Basque nationalism is a movement with roots in Carlism: the Basques supported the Carlists during the wars to retain their 'fuero' (medieval laws of the kingdom of Navarre defining the position of the king, the nobility and the judicial procedures and constitution). The Spanish Government alienated the Basques by revoking part of the fueros after the third Carlist War which lasted until 1876. The Spanish Civil War of 1936–39 and subsequent rule by Franco were seen by the Basques as another crusade against their independence.

In 1961 a small group of Basque nationalists formed an armed separatist group called Euskadi Ta Askatasuna (Basque Homeland and Freedom) — ETA — and turned to terrorism. Their violence continues today. They fought for independence from Francoist Spain until Franco died in 1975. In 1978, when Spain regained democracy and autonomy was restored to some of the Basque areas, the Basques in Navarre did not succeed in becoming a sovereign nation-state. This could only happen if the people and the institutions of Navarre gave their support but this has not yet happened, as Navarre's ties with the Basque Country are highly contested.

Today approximately seven million Basques live in the Basque territories. The Basques are said to be descendants of people who predate even the earliest Indo-European invasions of Europe. They retain a unique blood group and a separate language — many claim this is due to their long history of isolation from other peoples. In Navarre the speaking of Basque has become a political issue.

Food is another identifying feature of Basque culture in Navarre, with the 20th century seeing the emergence in San Sebastian (a seaside town near the French border) of men-only food clubs known as gastronomic societies. The tapas available in the bars are certainly tantalising, as are seafood dishes of cod, hake and cuttlefish, and the beef specialties offered in many restaurants.

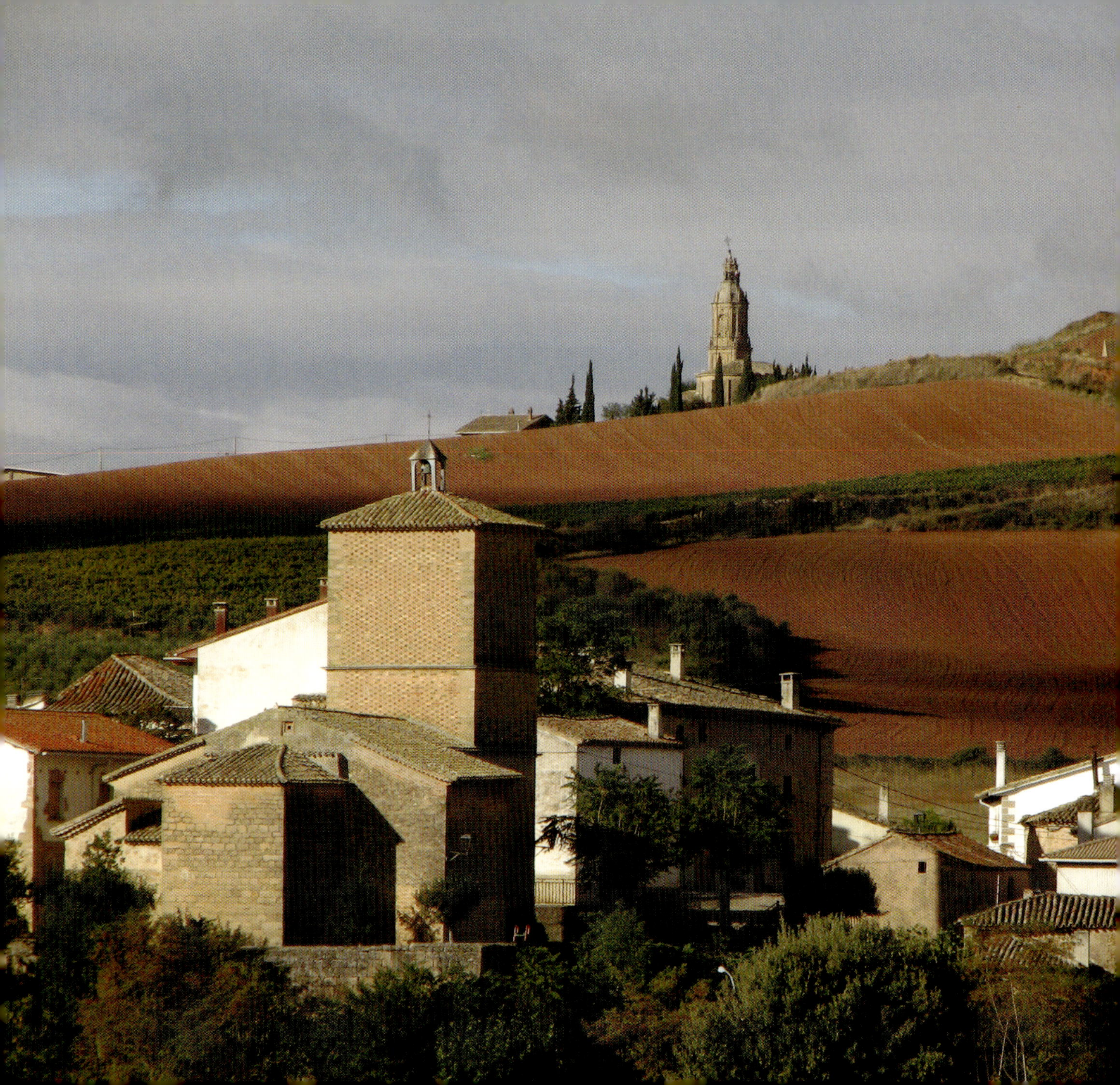

We visit the small, quiet town of Azqueta with its many attractive doorways and colourful flower boxes. From here we can see the town of Villamayor de Monjardín, dominated by the elegant tower of the 12th century San Andrés church. The town is built on higher ground and overlooks a patchwork of mixed farming land where tractors busily plough the rich red fields or spray from tanks a 'smelly' fertiliser. On top of the hill in Villamayor are the ruins of Castillo de San Esteba (St Stephen's Castle).

The interior of the San Andrés church is cool and austere. There is no coloured glass in its windows, the light is diffused through opaque panes and settles on three beautiful statues placed on a wall behind the altar. We sit awhile in peace and contemplation taking time to reflect on our week of walking

Others pray for such peace, as in a prayer by St Theresa: 'May today there be peace within … and allow your soul the freedom to sing, dance, praise and love.'

Our stillness is disturbed by the noisy arrival of the mobile shop. Many small country villages in Spain are dependent on these vans to supply a variety of supplies.

Prior to entering Villamayor we are fascinated by the 13th century Fountain of the Moors, Fuente de Los Moros. It is a square, covered structure built into a hill with an open, double-arched front wall decorated in a Mozarabic style, an exotic style that was developed by the Christians during the years of Muslim control. Inside, steps lead down to a rectangular pool fed by spring water dripping from one corner. The water in this pool slowly overflows into a square well at its centre. Many pilgrims find the pool a soothing place in which to soak tired feet.

The relaxed, easy camaraderie among pilgrims continues; in a *pelota* court in Villamayor we share a picnic with the same French Canadian couple we shared accommodation with in Orisson — still together on their honeymoon despite the snores.

Pelota is a ball game where you use your hand, a racket or a bat to hit a ball against a wall. Bats can vary in length and can be made of wood or basketry. It is played by two teams separated by a line on the ground or a net. Traced to ancient cultures, it is played widely in the Basque Country, and also in Ireland and America. Walls of a church or town hall are often incorporated into the building of a pelota court.

The walk to Los Arcos from Villamayor is 12 km on an open pebbly track that creeps across the undulating farmland. We are joined by a young group from Portugal, and chat as we walk through the rich brown tilled fields, past olive trees, vineyards and ancient hilltop ruins. Bare hills dotted with wind farms line the horizon. Through its many wind farm projects, Navarre is planning to generate much of its energy from renewable sources.

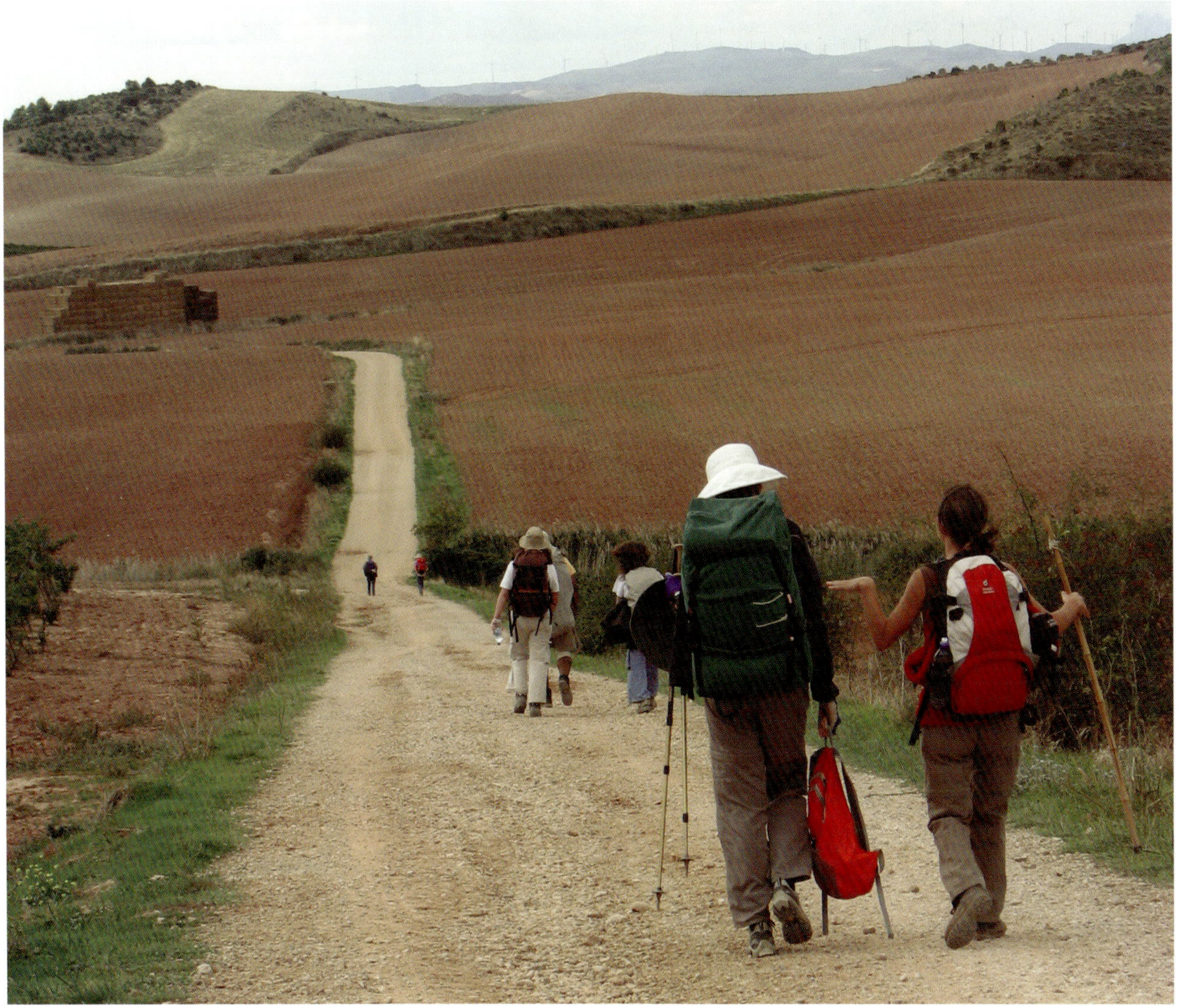

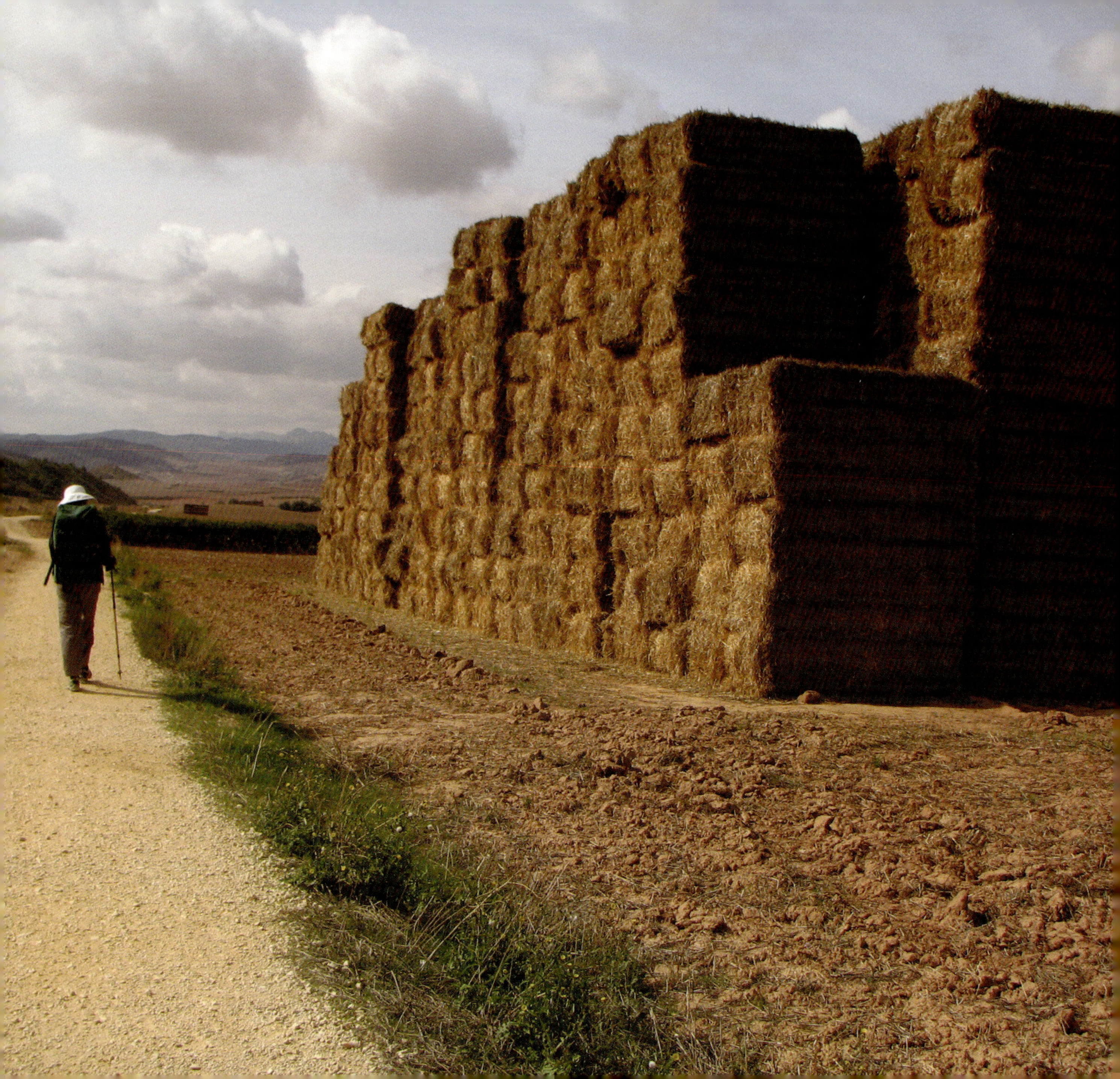

The track to Los Arcos seems endless, its red outline meandering across the bare and undulating countryside, not a farmhouse or a farmer in sight. Even the occasional pilgrim passing us, or glimpsed way ahead, has disappeared.

Our young group from Portugal decide to rest in the shade of a haystack. These enormous structures are numerous and glow in the golden afternoon sunshine. With no other buildings in sight, they offer some feeling of warmth and reassurance in an otherwise stark environment. We are tempted to stop but with 12 km still to go we need to continue.

Further on, resting at the 5 km waymarker to Los Arcos, we cannot believe there are so many footsteps to go. Surely not, we think, there must be a mistake. Maybe the waymarker has been moved and we have taken the wrong road.

This is the first time an uneasiness descends upon us. We are silent and alone. As we walk on, our eyes strain to reveal our surroundings which grow dim and unwelcoming with the lengthening shadows. The afternoon sun lowers rapidly towards the horizon and the air cools.

At last, around a slight rise, we come across one building, then another. Our dusty track becomes a road and more buildings appear. Our mood lightens as we enter the local square and join familiar faces. Interestingly, many of us compare notes about the town that would not appear.

TO LOS ARCOS

We meet up with our two walkers from Holland who look so well and relaxed after three months of walking. Sitting with us are two lively couples from Ireland who are trying to soak up the last warming rays of the sun. They are not the only ones as we are joined by a group of small kittens who take advantage of the warm pavement and any morsels of food we toss them. The *vino blanco seco* (dry white wine) and a chat are very welcome after the endless track to Los Arcos.

From our hotel window we look out onto the 12th century Iglesia de Santa Maria de los Arcos (Church of St Mary of the Arches), a church which harmoniously mixes architectural styles from Romanesque to Gothic, Baroque and Classical. It has a splendid Romanesque bell tower, and inside there is a magnificent Gothic cloister. The building's warm glow in the late afternoon light soothes us, as does the periodic ringing of the church bells.

Los Arcos is a crossroads town straddling the busy main east-west highway — a noisy town with several bus route connections. Out of Los Arcos the Camino leaves Navarre and enters La Rioja, a region famous for its wines. Two more regions, Castilla y León and Galicia, will be traversed before reaching Santiago de Compostela.

Tomorrow we reach Logroño where we temporarily break our walk by catching a bus to Burgos, León and then Pedrafita near O'Cebreiro to rejoin the Camino. Walking the flat plains of the *meseta* and the steep climb out of León are avoided and we have time to spend a few days exploring the historic cities of Burgos and León.

TO LOGROÑO AND BURGOS

On our way to Burgos, we are pleased to see the Camino close to the bus route and our thoughts go out to our fellow walkers. We also discover that many pilgrims use public transport to travel in and out of large cities, even joining our bus.

Burgos is large, crowded, and extremely noisy. Pilgrims who do not come in by bus are confronted by a bedlam of traffic and a long walk through industrial and suburban areas to reach the city's old centre. The route can also be ill defined, however, there are wonderful brass shell waymarkers embedded in the pavement throughout the historic precinct.

Dominated by Spain's greatest Gothic cathedral, Burgos is an elegant city well worth spending an extra day to explore. Within the historic precinct you can stroll through lovely gardens, along river promenades and enjoy the wines of Castilla, which are reported to be among the finest in the world.

Burgos was occupied by the Romans, the Visigoths and, briefly in the 8th century, the Arabs with Alfonso III the Great, King of Leon, reconquering the region in the middle of the 9th century. He built many castles for the defence of Christendom and the region came to be known as Castile, the 'land of the castles'.

It was originally a strategic fortress town. The name 'Burgos' comes from the Visigoths, and means 'consolidated walled villages'. It was built in 884 as an outpost of the expanding Christian empire and then became the capital of the Kingdom of Castile in the 10th century. It was an important stop for pilgrims on their way to Santiago and also the centre of trade between the Bay of Biscay and the south of Spain.

Burgos has been the scene of many wars against the Moors, between León and Navarre, between Castile and Aragon and in the Peninsular War against Napoleonic France. In the 19th century there was a further battle during the Carlist wars, and in the Spanish Civil War Burgos was the base of General Franco's Nationalist government.

Our bus deposits us close to the cathedral precinct — it is only a short walk across the Puente Santa Maria over the Rio Arlanzón, through the park which lines its banks, then under the ornate 14th century Arco de Santa Maria and into the elegant Plaza Fernando, the cathedral square. The cathedral is a truly magnificent sight, confronting, as it is one of the largest cathedrals in Spain. It entirely dominates the Old Quarter and the *plaza*, which is lined by two and three-storey houses notable for their glassed-in balconies (*galerias*) similar to those more often associated with some seaside towns.

TO LOGROÑO AND BURGOS

The cathedral is a Gothic giant which replaced a modest Romanesque church. It was begun in 1221 and took over 300 years to complete, embracing many architectural styles, including the Mozarabic. Its principal western façade, facing Santa Maria Square, has richly decorated twin towers reaching 84 m in height and topped by octagonal spires covered in open stonework traceries. This façade is three storeys high. The ground floor has three ogival entrances (pointed curved arches) with rectangular openings. On the second storey there is a fine, delicately carved rose window. Two double-arched ogival windows are found on the third storey with eight intercolumnar spaces, in each of which there is a statue on a pedestal. Above these is a balustrade of letters carved in stone forming the inscription, 'Pulchra es et deora', meaning 'Thou art beautiful and graceful'. In the centre of this balustrade is a statue of the Virgin Mary. The Gothic embellishments, the spires with their ornate decoration and the innumerable objects sculptured all over the cathedral's surface create a wonderful fantasy — evocative and elaborate. The cathedral is surrounded by an equally lovely maze of medieval streets so it is no wonder this Old Quarter has been declared a World Heritage site.

Burgos Cathedral is the burial place of the 11th century warrior Rodrigo Diaz de Vivar, known as El Cid Campeador, and his wife Jimena. El Cid was born in the nearby town of Vivar, and a large statue of him on his famous warhorse is located near the cathedral.

Epic tales, songs and poems about his exploits abound; some are factual, others legendary. Certainly, he was a remarkable warrior, military leader and administrator who commanded respect from both the Christians (who gave him the title 'Campeador', meaning 'champion') and the Moors (his title 'El Cid' is derived from Arabic, and means 'Chief' or 'Lord'). El Cid remains a heroic figure who conquered all against huge odds.

Of minor nobility, El Cid was educated in the Castilian royal court serving the prince, who became Sancho II following the death of his father, Ferdinand I the Great. After Sancho was killed El Cid became Chief General to the new king, Alfonso VI, only to be expelled from Castile by Alfonso, supposedly due to a falling out over suspicions held by El Cid and others that Sancho had been murdered by Alfonso. El Cid continued fighting during the early years of what is known as the Reconquista — a program by the Christians which lasted for over 700 years to reconquer modern Portugal and Spain from the Moors. During this time he married Alfonso's niece Jimena and had three children. He was exiled from Castile once more for making an unauthorised expedition into Granada in southern Spain and then went on to fight as a mercenary for both the Christians and the Moors.

Nearing the age of fifty, El Cid succeeded in taking the Mediterranean town of Valencia after a three-year siege, and although he ruled it in the name of Alfonso, he in fact created his own independent Christian/Moorish kingdom. Upon his death in 1099, his wife continued to rule, but needed to enlist assistance from Alfonso to withstand a siege by the Arab Almoravids, who were invading Spain. The family escaped back to Burgos when Valencia was captured in 1109 and the town returned to Moorish hands for another 125 years.

Directly behind the cathedral on the higher side of the Camino, steep steps lead up from the Plaza Santa Maria to the 15th century Iglesia de San Nicolas with its wondrously detailed wooden entrance doors. These steps deter many of the tourists and create a quiet and peaceful place to sit and enjoy looking out onto the cathedral.

Back on the fringe of the Plaza Santa Maria, and under a cool leafy tree, we savour a tasty mushroom omelette, a glass of refreshing wine, re-read our walking guide and marvel at the intricate decoration of the cathedral's western façade before us.

TO LEÓN

Today we travel for three hours by bus across the *meseta* (plains) from Burgos to León over a distance of 182.4 km — a journey which takes eight days to walk.

We are comforted when the Camino is close by, and we watch those upon it with fondness. At other times, when the path is swallowed up by the vast empty landscape, we experience a sadness at losing a familiar friend, but a friend we will find again at León.

It is a bleak, inhospitable yet impressive region where winter winds are dry and cold and summer winds are dry and hot. Therefore, walking the *meseta* in the spring (March/April) or autumn (late September/October) has advantages:

The journey to León across the bleak, inhospitable *meseta* was best travelled by bus.

the weather is kinder and there are fewer pilgrims. Today is a mild and sunny autumn day and the searing heat of summer has gone. We are pleased our fellow pilgrims will not have to walk this section during the cool of the nights to avoid travelling during the hottest part of the day.

The *meseta* occupies about half of Spain's land area framed by the Cantabrian Mountains on the north and the Sierra Morena Ranges on the south. The Camino Route between Burgos and León crosses the *meseta* and through the autonomous community of Castilla y León.

It can be a lonely walk passing endless fields of wheat, barley or oats. There is little shade and often few towns and water fonts. The days can be long, challenging and strenuous. At times the scenery is flat, featureless and monotonous, yet it can be, as many pilgrims told us, inspiring, wondrous, peaceful and calm; an exalting experience.

The city of León originated in 68 AD as a Roman military settlement. Built on the banks of the Rio Bernesga, its name was derived from its occupants, the Roman legionnaires.

Its history includes occupation by the Roman garrison, then the conquering and re-conquering Visigoths, the Moors and finally the Christians. Each of these groups left its mark, creating a city with an extraordinary historic and artistic heritage; it is a marriage of many styles — from Roman to Romanesque, Gothic, Renaissance, Neo-Gothic, and modern. Today it is a thriving city.

The town's ancient walls date back to Roman times and were built in a rectangle around the original settlement. The Camino enters the Old Town through Puerta Moneda, one of four remaining old gateways. Over the centuries many modifications have been made, and today medieval walls sit atop remnants of an earlier time. Buildings too have used the walls as part of their construction; some are even nestled within the structure.

One such building is the Real Basílica de San Isodoro, nicknamed the 'Sistine Chapel of Spanish Romanesque'. Napoleon's troops sacked this church early in the 19th century, but despite breaking into the vaults and stealing jewellery and gold, the artwork was not vandalised — what was left remains one of the greatest treasures of Romanesque art in Spain, if not Europe. Depicting biblical stories, these 12th-century frescoes cover the vaults and arches in the Panteón Real, in which lie over 40 burial vaults of León and Castilla royalty. A museum within the Basílica displays what remains of the gold and jewellery, and from it there is access to the cloisters.

During a Holy Year pilgrims unable to travel on to Santiago due to ill health could receive a plenary indulgence (a full remission of all one's sins) by walking through the Door of Forgiveness in this church, or a partial remission of sins at other times.

Also worth seeing is the medieval agricultural calendar near the church's main entrance and the sculptural work around the right-hand entrance. It was created by Maestro Mateo, whose genius is also seen at the cathedral in Santiago de Compostela.

The city of León's Old Town.

The Plaza de San Marcelo.

The Camino passes through the medieval streets of León's Old Town, once again waymarked by elegant brass scallop shells embedded in the pavement. We are warmed and proud at seeing the scallop shells once more. Their presence is a friendly symbol of our amazing walk of discovery, our exciting journey.

With our accommodation close to the Old Town, we explored its environs daily. On the first morning we walked to the Plaza de San Marcelo, with its 12th century Iglesia San Marcelo. The morning was cool and overcast, and already old men were standing in groups chatting. In a similar way the large fat pigeons clustered together on the ledges of the central fountain. Artists sitting on their tiny stools were engrossed in capturing the scene. Overhead, large trees still in their summer dress formed a dark green canopy, creating a sheltered place for us to sit and watch.

Antonio Gaudí's neo-Gothic Casa Botines.

A sculpture of Gaudí.

On the northern edge of the Plaza de San Marcelo stands Antonio Gaudí's neo-Gothic Casa Botines. Built in the late 1800s of grey granite with a black slate roof, it was completed in ten months. It is one of only three Gaudí buildings outside Catalonia and consists of four floors, plus a basement and attic. It has four corner towers and its windows are identical on all four sides, decreasing in size as they go up the building. There was controversy over the way the building was structurally designed — the local engineers did not approve of Gaudí's use of continuous lintels for the foundation. Rumours abounded that the building was going to fall down. Today, the building is still sound, and in the 1990s it underwent a full restoration reflecting Gaudí's original design. A Spanish bank currently occupies the building.

Interestingly, in the early 1950s there was discussion about restoring the sculpture of St George and the Dragon over the main entrance door (it had fallen into disrepair) or perhaps replacing it with the patron saint of León. Agreement was finally reached to restore the original sculpture, and when it was removed a lead pipe was found in its pedestal. The pipe contained floor and elevation plans signed by Gaudí and the owners,

The restored sculpture of St George and the Dragon.

news reports from the period, manuscripts relating to the property, the Certificate of Completion of Construction, some sketches by Gaudí and drawings of details of the edifice. From these the names of all the artisans who worked on the building were discovered.

A sculpture of Gaudí, sketching, can be seen sitting on a bench facing his special building. Such life-like sculptures are found in many of the larger Spanish cities. They add to the pleasure of visiting these wonderful sites.

The building to the right of Casa Botines and facing the square, is the Renaissance Placio de los Guzmanes, built in the 17th century. It has a lovely façade, with square corner towers, and within there is a columned patio. Presently it is the seat of the Provincial Delegation of León.

In the centre of the Old Town lies its Gothic gem, the 13th century Catedral de Santa Maria, facing the Plaza Regal. The cathedral is renowned for its extraordinary 2000 square metres of French-inspired stained glass windows, installed between the 13th and the 16th centuries. Aside from the three huge rose windows, there are some thirty kaleidoscope windows around the main body of the church. As an interesting aside, a great deal of the cathedral's gold and silver was melted down to finance the Peninsular War against Napoleon between 1808 and 1814.

This is truly a wondrous 13th century Gothic cathedral, especially at the time we see it, with its stone walls illuminated by the morning light. As the nearby street sculpture of a father and son gaze at the cathedral in awe, we sit at a café sipping a warm cup of coffee and savouring the moment. Not for long, however, as we are eager to see what lies behind the three ogival-styled entrances.

Upon entering there is an explosion of colour which seems to engulf us and fill the tall arched inner space; the magical light grows brighter one moment and darker the next as the light changes outside. There is a fairytale quality created by the mass of stained glass. This is a cathedral able to tell stories — a picture book with pages of stained glass. No wonder it is known as 'Pulchra Leonina' (the 'House of Light'), for it is pure, polished and refined, its interior unencumbered by broad pillars, allowing the stained glass windows to show their full splendour. It is magical in a similar way to Sainte Chapelle in Paris.

TO LEÓN

The richness of religious art within the cathedral is captivating, as in the stone carving we find in a quiet corner. The figures are gathered around a sarcophagus and glow in a soft grey light. It is a powerful scene, evoking a sense of serenity and love. They appear like guardian angels expressing their love and care.

A belief in guardian angels can be traced through antiquity and an angel doctrine is discernible in the Bible. In the Old Testament they were Ministers of God, as when God says to Moses, 'My angel shall go before thee' (Exodus 32:34). In the New Testament we relate our belief in 'our' guardian angels in the quote from Hebrews 1:14, 'Are they not all ministering spirits sent to save for the sake of those who are to inherit salvation.'

We are certainly finding 'earthly' angels on the Way. At times when we need some assistance or guidance, they appear, real people who happen to be there at the right moment — the taxi driver we come across when we felt weary towards the end of a day's walk, who drove us the last couple of kilometres to our destination. The fellow walker who speaks Spanish and rings ahead and books our accommodation for the entire first section. Trying to book our own accommodation has proven difficult for us because our Spanish is very poor and the English of those who run the small hotels is even worse. Being slow walkers, having our accommodation booked is a great relief.

At León we are helped with our bookings once more and with the very confusing bus trip to join the Camino again. This requires changing buses and knowing where to disembark to walk into O'Cebreiro. All is taken care of by our very lovely hotel receptionist. We were overcome by her kindness and thanked her with a card addressed to 'our angel'.

Other pilgrims talk of similar experiences, of receiving kindnesses or assistance along the Way. Walking the Camino allows you to be receptive to the protective and supportive ways of these earthly angels, and to be open to the love and care of your fellow pilgrims.

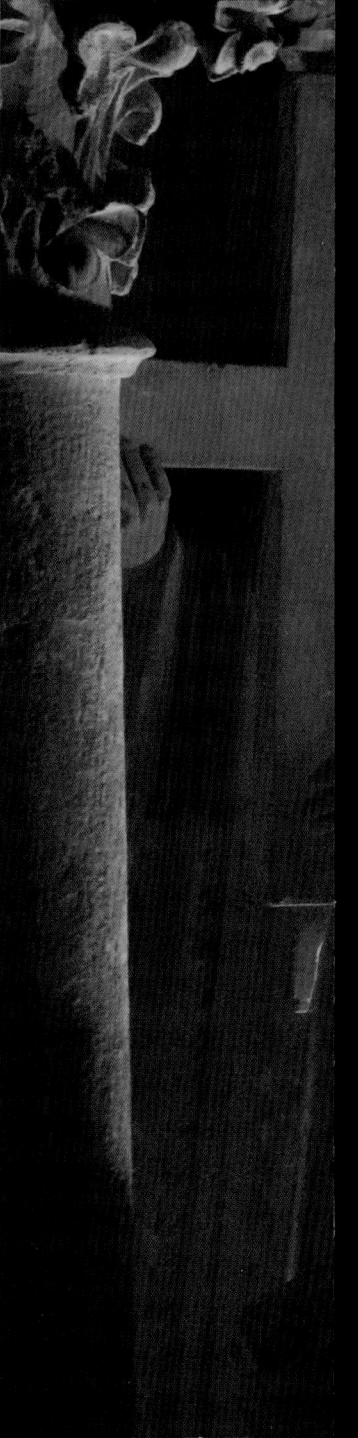

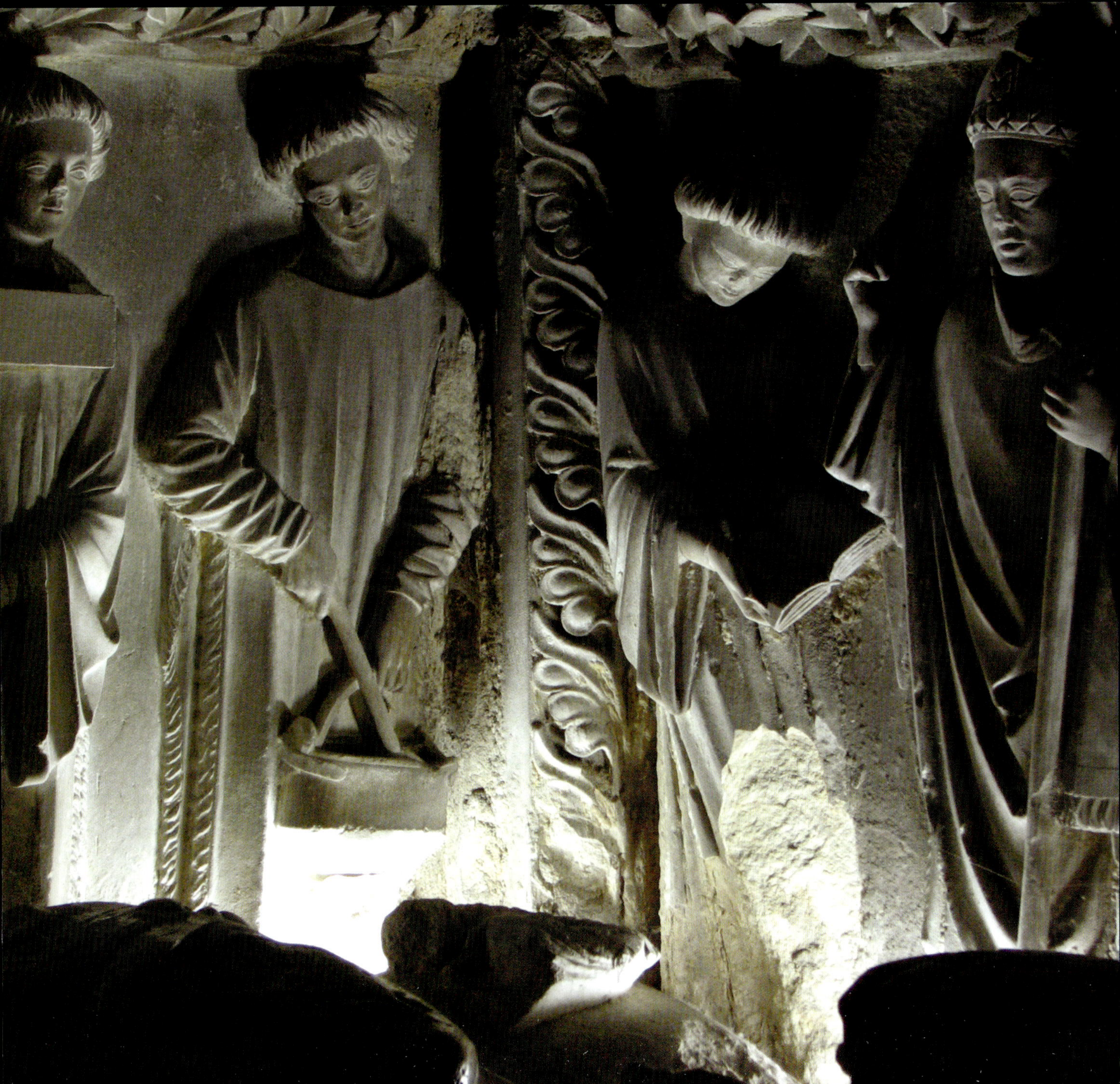

The Chapel of San Marcos.

On the northern edge of the Old Town and abutting the tree-lined Rio Bernesga near the 16th century stone pilgrims' bridge Puente de Rio Bernesga is the Hostal de San Marcos, now a *parador*, a five-star hotel. Seen through glass doors to the right of its entrance is a courtyard with cloistered galleries. These have lovely *artesonado* ceilings: decorative wooden panelling in Mudejar/Muslim style. Built in the 12th century as a pilgrim hospital, it later became home to the Knights of Santiago. In the 16th century the *hostal* was remodelled, and a highly elaborate plateresque façade was added. The building is long and opens onto the wide paved Plaza San Marcos, which has a chapel and museum at one end.

Outside, facing the *hostal*, a street sculpture of a pilgrim sits, resting against a column, eyes closed, his sandals discarded. We are joined by a French Canadian woman whom we met earlier on the Way and share with the pilgrim a sense of thanksgiving.

We say goodbye to the wonderful city of León and its Old Town, where so many historical periods and architectural styles sit effortlessly side by side. Three days have been barely enough time to see it all — the ancient Roman ruins, the magical stained glass of the Gothic cathedral, the Neo-Gothic fairytale style of Gaudí, the rich Romanesque art treasures in the Real Basílica de San Isodoro and the highly detailed plateresque façade of the Hostal de San Marcos.

Mingling through it all, the modern influence sits happily with the city's extraordinary historical and artistic past.

León is the last major city before the Camino climbs into the *sierras* (mountains) that separate the territories of Castilla y León from Galicia, introducing pilgrims to a change in climate, landscape, language and people. The countryside around the city is a fertile plain surrounded by woods, orchards and meadows. It is an area well known throughout Spain for its meat, cheeses, butter, hams and sausages.

Street sculptures in the Old Town.

TO O'CEBREIRO

Another three-hour journey by bus takes us to Pedrafita near O'Cebreiro, a distance of 162.7 km which would take six days to walk. We pass the relatively flat and solitary section at the beginning where there are few villages and water fonts, before heading towards the mountain range and O'Cebreiro, where the weather can be unpredictable.

Between Rabanal and Acebo, before Ponferrada, the highest pass on the Way is crossed at Ponto Alto (1515 m). If walking, care needs to be taken on the downhill path after crossing the pass.

At Ponferrada, where the bus route and the Camino cross, is the mammoth 12th century Castillo de Los Templarios. Ponferrada came under the protectorate of the Knights Templar in 1180. The Castillo was finished in 1282 but abandoned 30 years later when the order was outlawed and disbanded by the Catholic Church.

The final climb of 31 km into wild Galicia and the lovely mountain hamlet of O'Cebreiro is the most taxing of the entire walk. The path runs through the beautiful Valcarce Valley, and walkers are rewarded with misty breathtaking views. Our bus journey ends at Pedrafita, where we enjoy lunch at a local café before walking into O'Cebreiro, a short distance away.

O'Cebreiro is the gateway to Galicia, another autonomous territory. In Galicia, rain can come at any time of the year and the temperatures are usually mild, except in the mountains. The forests and endless hills return — the chestnuts, oaks, then pines and finally eucalyptuses. It is rich dairy and farming country: the common crops are potato, corn, cabbage and a leafy green vegetable called *greles*, which is made into a soup. The Camino now makes an undulating descent to Compostela, the Camino's lowest point (260 m), through innumerable hamlets and stone walls — the inheritance practices here have led to continual division of land.

The town's traditional houses, known as *pallozas*.

TO O'CEBREIRO

Galicia is also the land of the Celts, even though it is the most forgotten of the seven Celtic nations — the others being Brittany, Scotland, Ireland, Wales, the Isle of Man and Cornwall. It has some of the oldest Celtic traditions, going back 2000 years, and the haunting music from Galician bagpipes (*gaitas*) can still be heard.

O'Cebreiro is a medieval town, a tiny wind-battered settlement of stone houses high above a patchwork quilt of green valleys and surrounded by spectacular mountains. It is the home of the ancient traditional houses known as *pallozas*, nine of which still remain. These dwellings were developed in pre-Roman times. They are constructed on an oval floor around which a one-metre-high stone wall rises to meet the conical roof of rye-thatch which keeps out the snow and rain. People and animals share the inside, which is divided into various rooms and has a hearth in the centre. The *pallozas* all face south and are built on a slant to improve drainage. They have small windows but no chimneys; the smoke filters up through the thatch.

This has always been an important place for pilgrims along the route. The church and adjoining *hostal* formed part of a monastic settlement that dates back to the 11th century. It was first assigned to French monks and then to the Benedictines, who remained until the 19th century. Part of the church, Iglesia de Santa Maria Real, dates back to the 9th century. In the 13th century a miracle is said to have occurred during a mass, when the wine and bread literally turned into the blood and flesh of Christ as they were being offered to a peasant. The 12th century statue of the Virgin Mary is said to have inclined her head at the miraculous event and she has remained in that position ever since. On 8 September each year some 30,000 pilgrims come to this church to celebrate the Virgin Mary and the chalice and paten (plate) of the miracle found inside.

It is inside the Iglesia de Santa Maria Real that we leave behind a favourite old French walking hat. We had attended a Pilgrims' Mass in the late afternoon, and had also become absorbed in this peaceful ancient place. The mystery of the chalice and paten, sitting in their protective glass case, the statue of the Virgin Mary with her head inclined, a small simple wooden statue of a pilgrim, the flowers and the many burning candles all added to the atmosphere. Outside, too, we had spent time exploring the old graveyard where rows of huge flat-cut rectangular slabs lay on the ground. It is not until we move on the next day that we realise we are missing 'the' hat, a special hat which we had bought in Paris.

From the window of our accommodation we look on to steep hills and valleys. Before us there is a sea of traditional grey slate roofs, with smooth tiles, circular in shape, that overlap each other like fish scales.

Our guardian angels are still looking out for us when we stop for lunch en route to Sarria. There on a hat stand was an almost identical hat, except this one was made in China! Upon enquiring about it and telling our story, we were told it had no owner, as it had been left behind some time ago. 'May we buy it?' we ask. 'No,' is the reply, 'you may have it.'

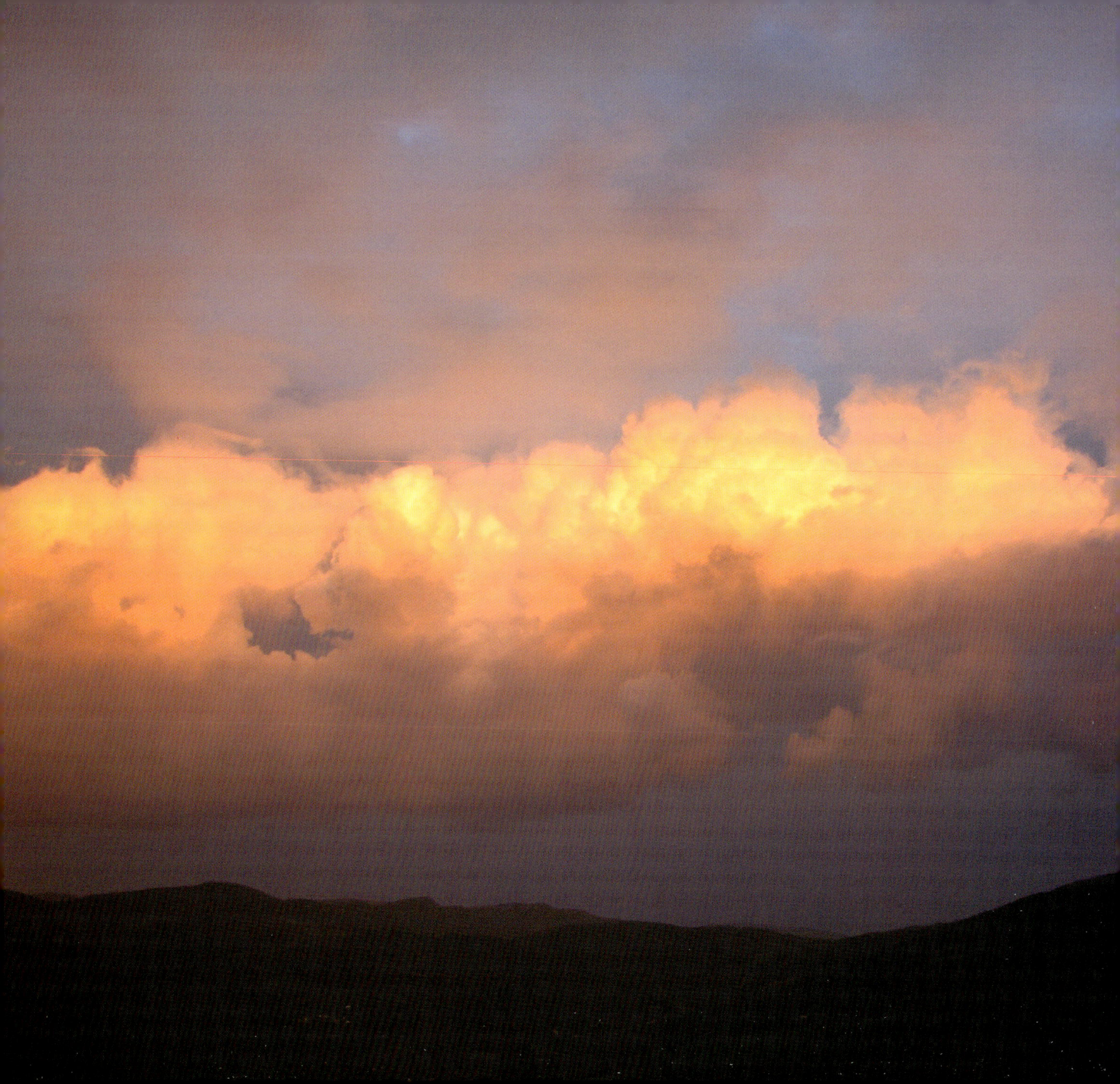

TO TRIACASTELA

A magical sunrise lights the clouds in golds and pinks as we leave O'Cebreiro.

It is a misty morning. There are beautiful views, enchanting hills, green and lush pastures, old granite churches, shady trees, countless hamlets, endless stone fences.

A couple, who had been sitting on our hotel steps the night before, speaking softly, mingling tears and caresses, walk ahead of us as we leave O'Cebreiro. They go hand in hand, their shells swinging side to side. We are all at peace.

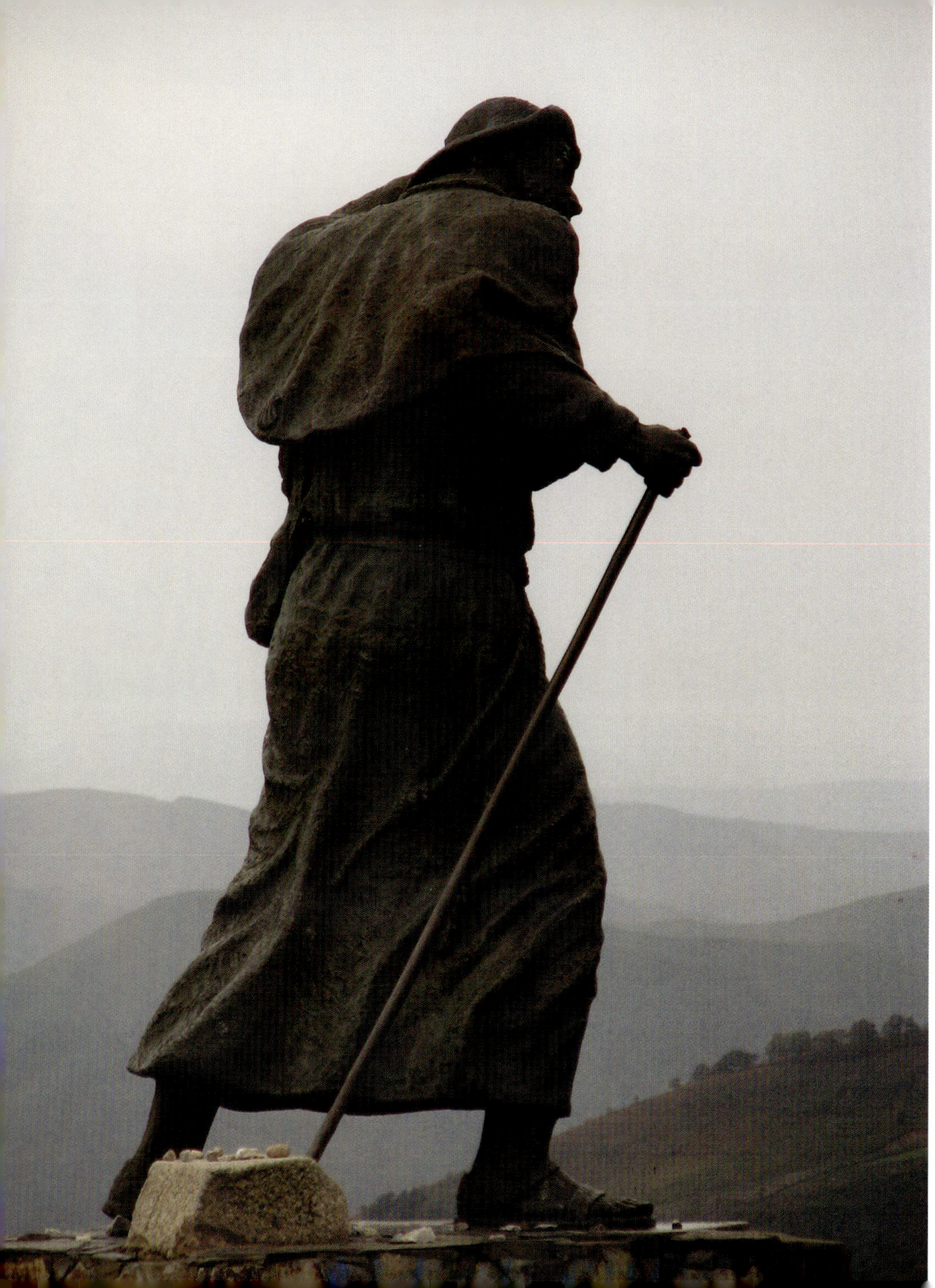

There are great views from the Pilgrim Statue on Alto San Roque, at 1270 m; a gradual descent to Santiago de Compostela lies ahead.

At Linares, while enjoying a coffee at a local bar, we discover an old wooden loom — it was in this region flax was grown for the linen trade.

Our walk along this section of the Camino is intertwined with that of a French Canadian artist. Conditioned to recording our reflections in words and through the lens of a camera, we are fascinated with what she saw and drew.

Like us, she captured the chapels, the crosses, the bare plains and the fields of sunflowers. But she also immortalised the little quirky moments that defined the journey like character lines on an old face — the pilgrim walking along knitting while kittens played with the trailing skeins of wool, the pain of a pilgrim's bandaged feet, a lonely dog curled up in the bleak protection of an ancient doorway, and the contentment of a warm cat asleep under a sheltering bush.

Later these sketches were made into small lino block prints, and it seems appropriate that the images had to be cut painstakingly into the linoleum like each individual footstep marking the miles of the Camino.

We are now in Galicia, where the westerly winds from the Atlantic meet the mountains … and there is rain, rain and more rain. The greys and greens, and the white buildings such as the *albergue* ahead, stand out brightly. It is a tranquil, peaceful scene, soft and gentle.

We are heading to Triacastela where pilgrims would each take a heavy stone from the local quarry and carry it to the lime kilns at Castañeda, four days walk away. The lime was used in the building of the Catedral de Santiago de Compostela. Triacastela, which means 'town of three castles' (none of which remains today), provides good accommodation and places to eat — before a magical day of walking beside the Rio Oribio.

Galicia has a distinctive language known as Galego that sounds like a mixture of Castilian Spanish and Portuguese. It was suppressed during the Franco years, but is now encouraged as the main local language and spoken widely. For the pilgrim it is very confusing, because it has different sounds and spellings from Spanish. Map reading becomes complicated when common Spanish words such as *plaza* become *praza*, or when an 'x' in Galego replaces the 'g' or 'j' and sounds like 'sch'.

Galicia is also culturally different from the rest of Spain, having been shaped by its inhabitants over the centuries. The Iron Age Celts appeared as long ago as 3000 BC. They were followed by the Romans, who gave the area its name, 'Gallaecia'. The Muslims came next although they had little influence on this part of Spain. The discovery of the tomb of St James in 815 AD had a large impact, creating a symbol for the Reconquista. After this period, Galicia remained untouched, an impoverished backwater controlled by the Catholic monarchs Fernando and Isabel, who supplanted its local language and traditions with Castilian ways. Not until the late 19th century was there a reawakening of Galician consciousness, known as Rexurdimento; however, the area then suffered greatly during Franco's rule (1939–75).

The mystical colours of Galicia: The greys of the old stone and slate; the greens of the lush rolling pastures, the mountains and forests, the shady trees, the dampness, the raindrops and the mist in the mornings; the blue of the skies when the weather clears; the old stone fences; the moss-covered crosses, the ancient churches and chapels, and the numerous hamlets. It is mystical, spiritual, nurturing and peaceful — a stage for the muses, the tellers of tales, the dreamers, the poets, the musicians … and for pilgrims, a place of reflection.

Ironically, Galicia was able to eventually become an autonomous region within Spain partly because of having been ignored for such a long period. Today it is still a rural region, with fishing its mainstay. Its long association with the sea, in particular its history of smuggling, has become an integral part of its folklore. In the same way the links with its Celtic past are seen in many rich and distinctive traditions.

There are reminders of the area's pagan past everywhere. Long before the discovery of St James' tomb, and before Christianity spread to Galicia, large numbers of pilgrims came to its western shores where the sun setting behind the water's edge was seen as the end of their ancient world (hence 'Finisterre').

TO SARRIA

On old paths and cart tracks crisscrossing the winding Rio Oribio, we walk over fallen chestnuts and under green and shady birch, oak, chestnut and poplar trees. The soil is dark and rich, all is damp, and moisture clings tenaciously to the foliage. Leaves twinkle like diamonds as the sun's rays penetrate these secret mystical places and settle on dewdrops. Lichen and small plants embed themselves into tree trunks and cover rock surfaces, creating fairy gardens. Among the ground plants protruding wondrously and triumphantly into the air are the most amazing mushrooms, like this one, ablaze in the brightest of colours.

Plants found along the Way have been used for centuries by pilgrims and the hospitals that cared for them — herbs to soothe blisters, fennel boiled in milk as an energy drink. Vinegar and salt mixed in cool water is still recommended for tired feet.

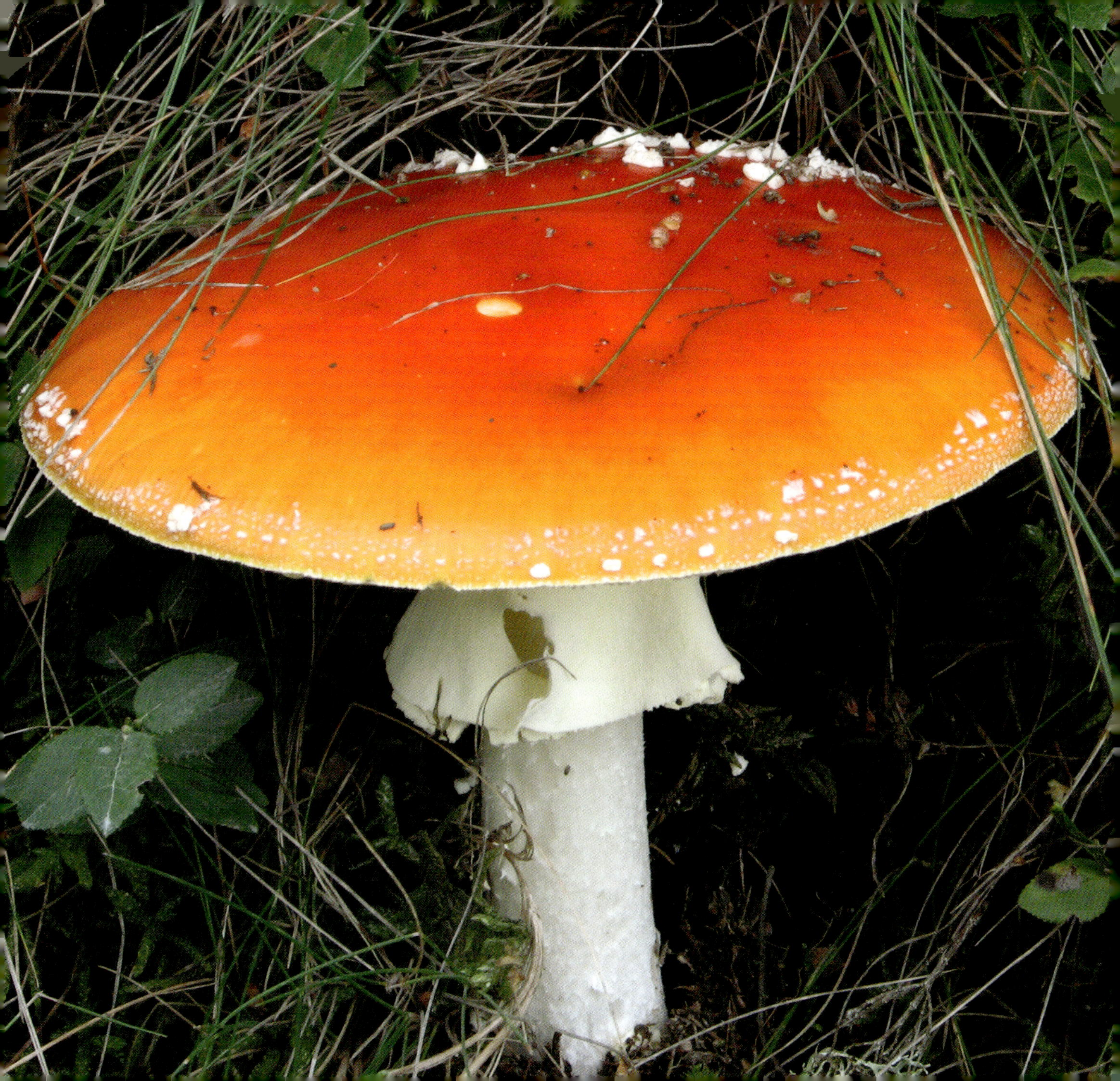

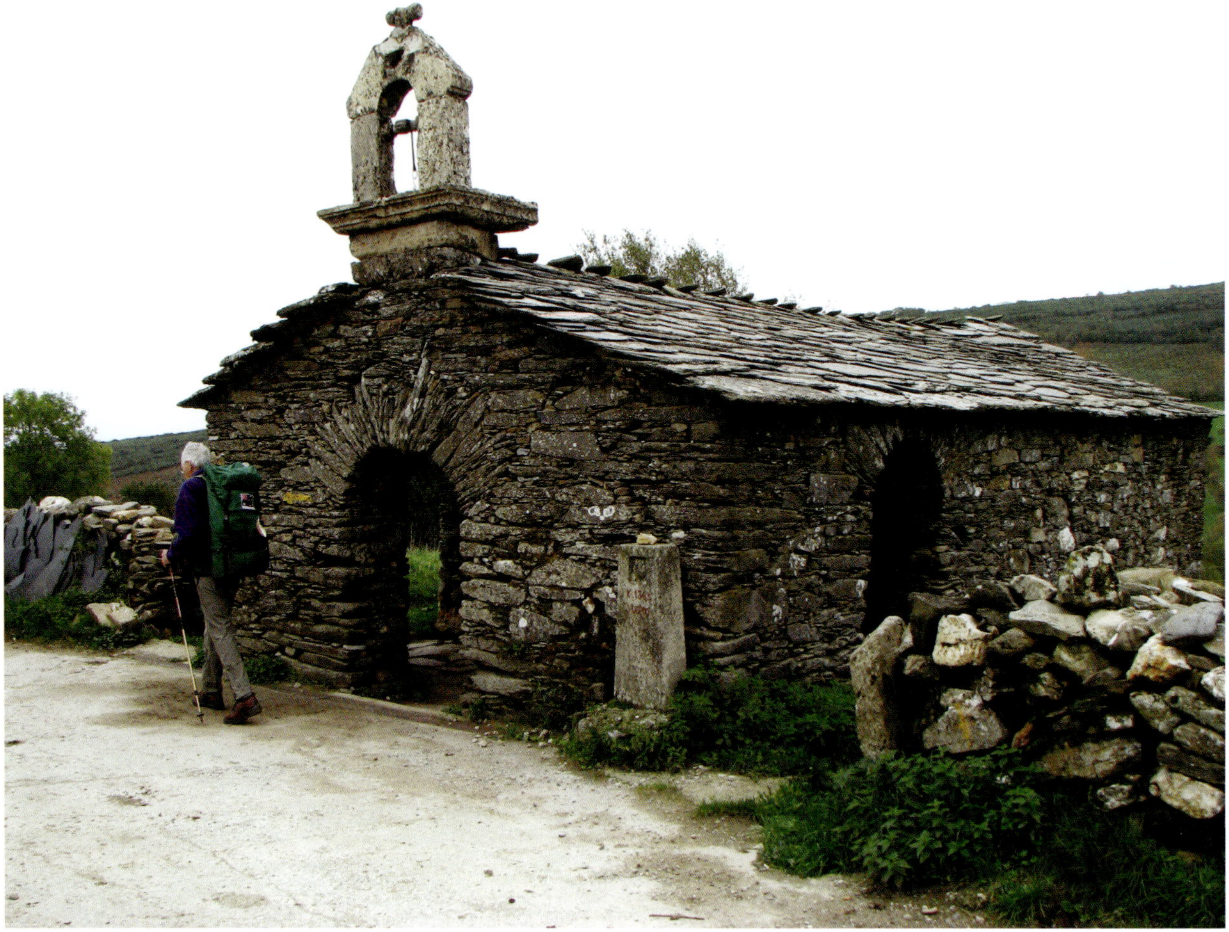

Past the grey granite and slate of the churches and chapels found in the numerous hamlets in this area, we come to the ancient stone mill and weir at San Cristobo on the Rio Oribio. It is a tranquil place — under tall leafy trees we are protected from the soft rain and listen to the sound of bubbling water. We feel an overwhelming desire not to hurry, to linger and absorb the atmosphere and history.

The Rio Oribio valley is truly beautiful; the greenness is at times overwhelming. Some of the hamlets are old and unkempt, and the Camino paths are sometimes clogged with mud and cow dung. Modern homes appear unexpectedly, many constructed in traditional ways.

Cattle, sheep, pigs and geese enjoy the rich green pastures of rural Galicia. Being a poor region, many of the men, young and old, have left to find employment elsewhere, leaving much of the farm work to be carried out by the women and the elderly. These are the people you pass on the Way, tending to their vegetables and animals, collecting chestnuts and mushrooms, storing the corn and maize for winter.

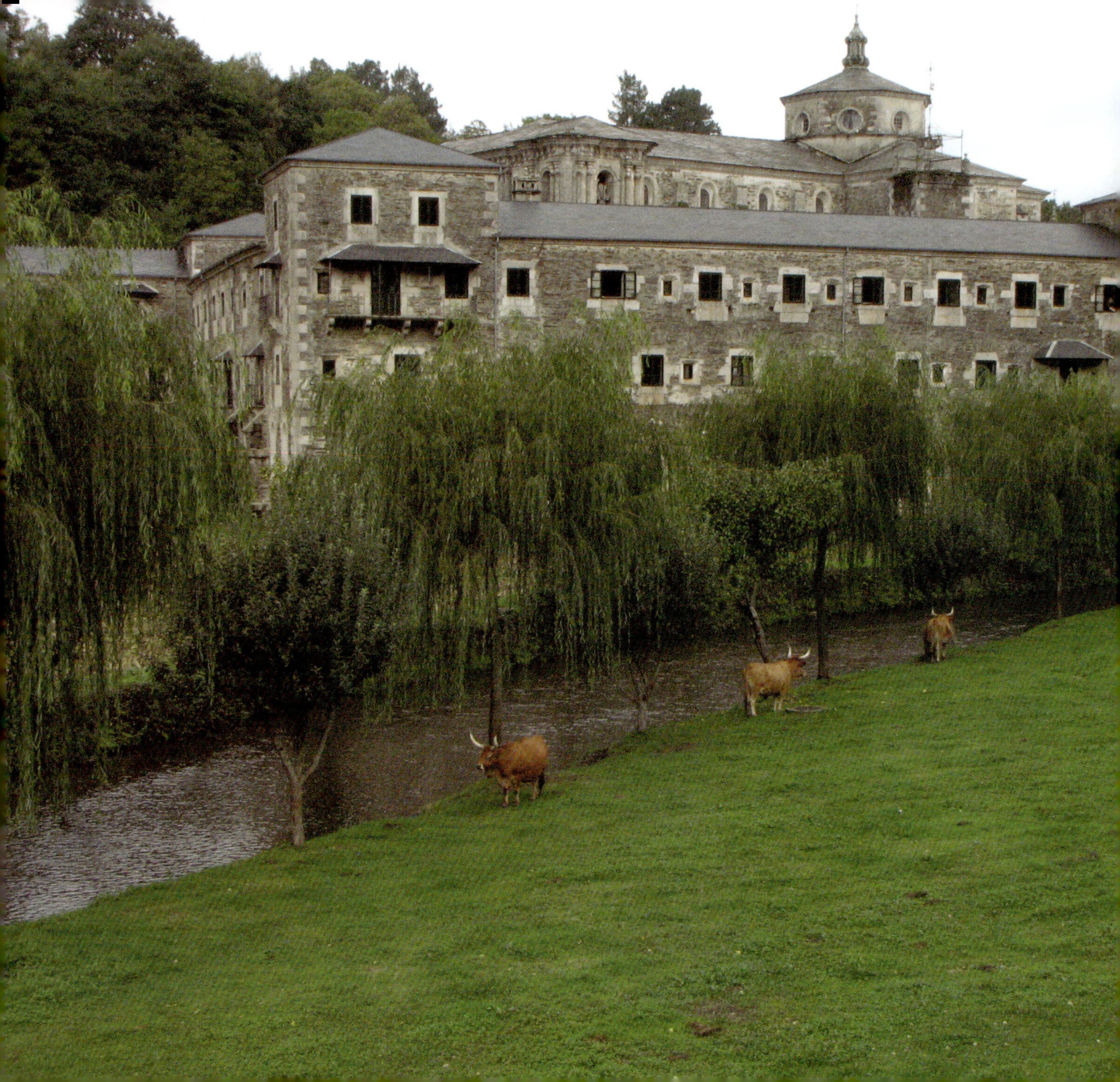

We are lulled into a quietened state by the peaceful 11-km morning walk from Triacastela. Our first sighting of Samos Monastery excited us, and further glimpses are tantalising, making us impatient to get there. Through breaks in the trees, this enormous building has been appearing on our right as we approach the town of Samos. It has been magical seeing the monastery for brief moments before being swallowed up once more by the vegetation or the meandering path as it wanders down to the valley floor.

Sitting proudly on the edge of the Rio Oribio overlooking grazing cattle and geese, the monastery is large and grey, looking formidable and overwhelming with the tall dark forest as its backdrop.

One of the oldest monasteries in Spain, San Xian de Samos was originally the site of a community of hermits favoured by the religious hierarchy. In the 6th century St Martin of Dumie began the building of the original monastery to further his promotion within the monastic world in Galicia (the date is confirmed by a Visigoth tablet). In the 10th century the traditional regime of the monastery was changed by St Benito (Benedict) of Nursia and it became a Benedictine monastery.

In the 12th century the monastery was rebuilt, but it was later destroyed by fire. In 1533 it was rebuilt in the Gothic style until fire struck again in 1951, destroying anything not made of stone — it left only the 18th century church unharmed. The whole complex was then lovingly rebuilt to its present style — a mixture of Romanesque, Gothic, Renaissance and Baroque.

Today, the monastery eclipses the small town of Samos. Within it there is an *albergue* offering some 90 beds for pilgrims (with fairly basic facilities).

Guided tours are run every day through various sections of the monastery. Attending vespers in the magnificent church is recommended.

The cloisters of San Xian de Samos and the gardens they overlook are exquisite as the afternoon light creates wonderful shadows. Nothing stirs, all is quiet. As is the case for many of the monasteries in Spain, very few monks live within this monastery's walls, and novices are few.

In the deeper shadows of the cloister we glimpse the fleeting figure of an elderly nun; she retreats into a doorway as we draw near. No contact can be made.

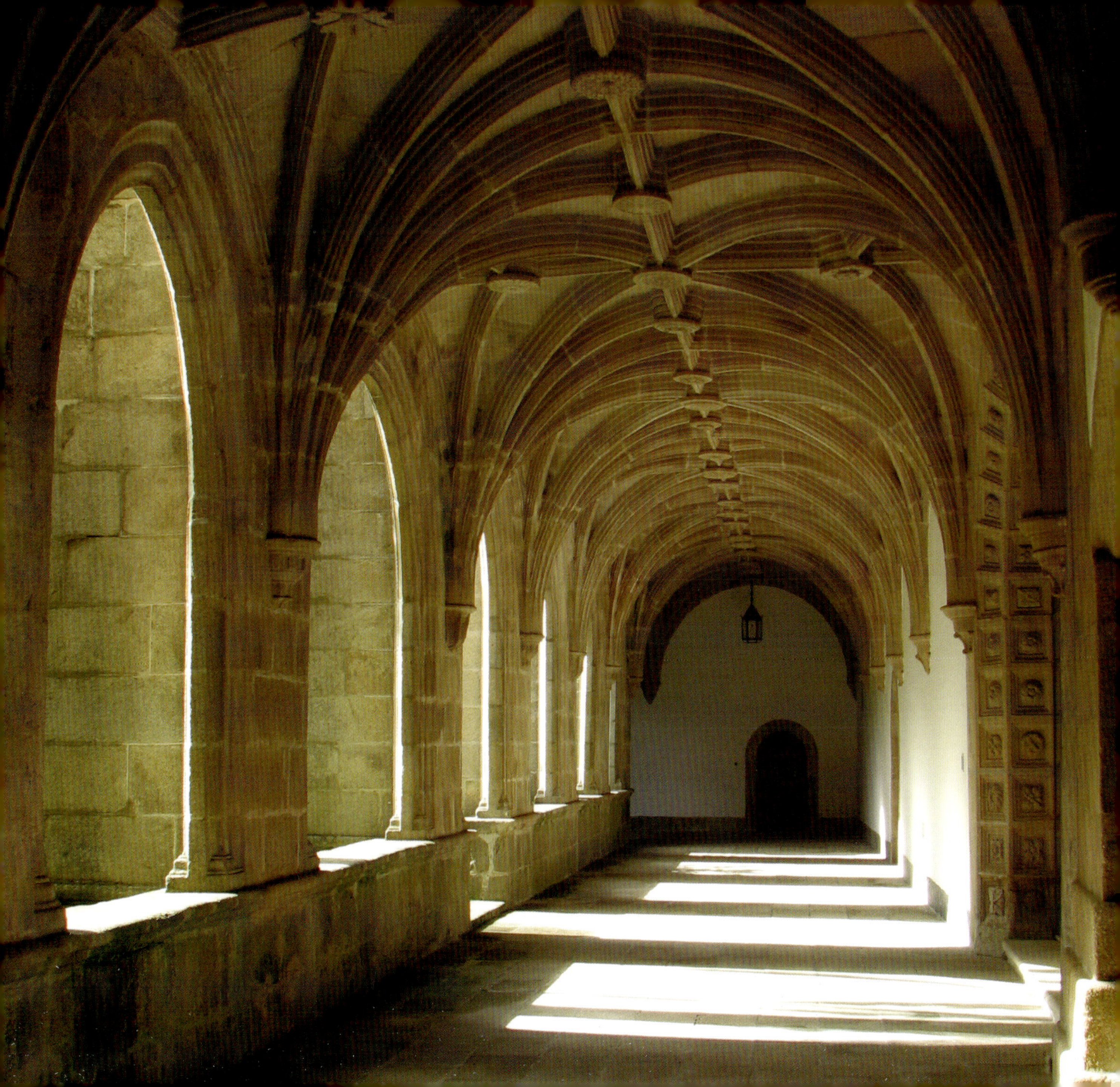

Sarria, our night's destination after Samos, has become an important starting point for pilgrims who have little time but wish to obtain their Compostela at Santiago. Being 111 km from Santiago, the town is well situated for these pilgrims to complete their minimum 100 km. We are aware of an increase in the number of pilgrims walking and also meet school groups along the Way.

Sarria was also an important centre for pilgrims in medieval times, boasting seven hospitals and many churches and monasteries to care for the travellers. In Sarria's old hilltop quarter we discover numerous ancient churches, stone crosses, a ruined 13th century fort and the attractive 13th century Convento de la Madalena.

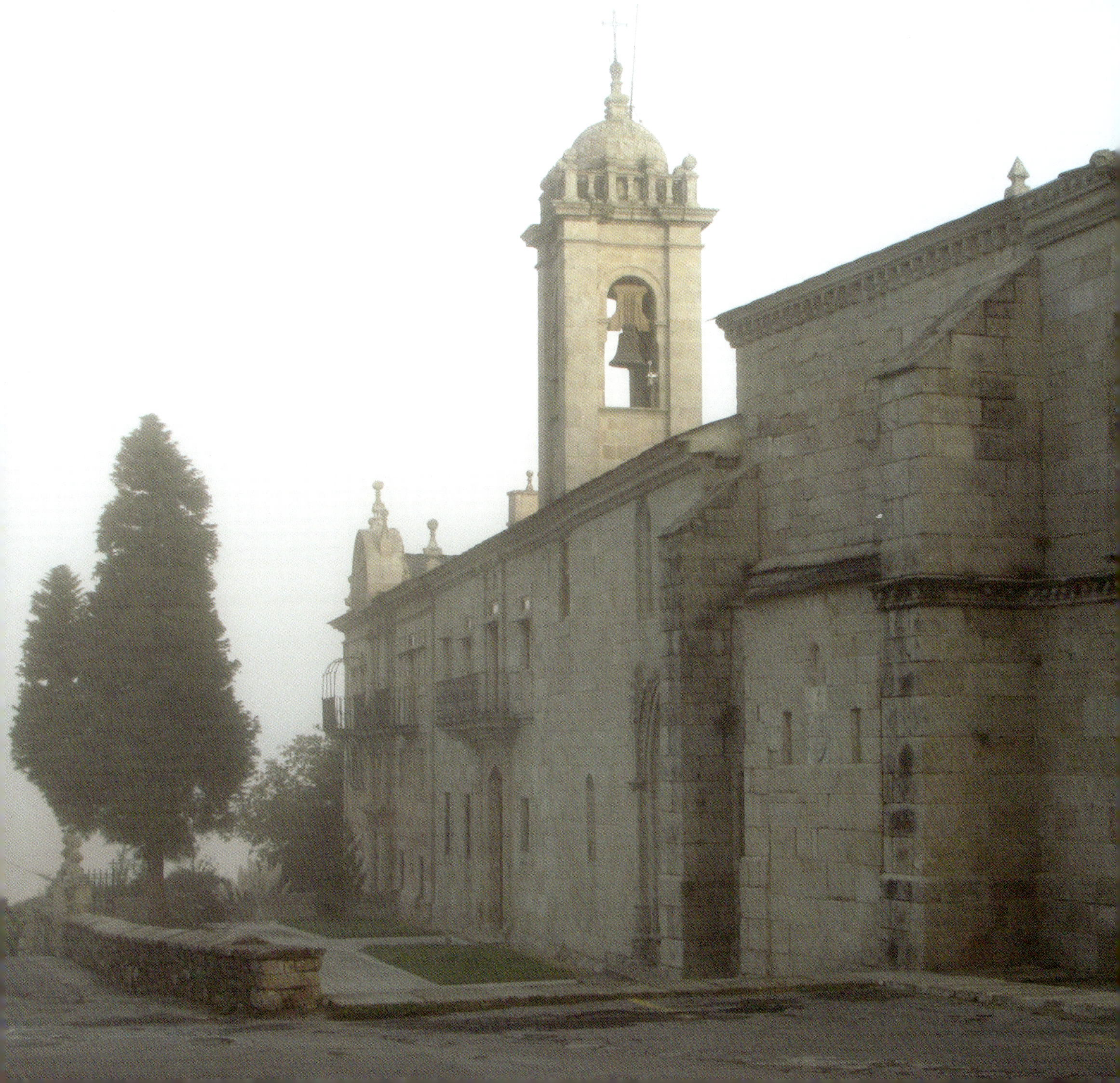

TO PORTOMARÍN

Leaving Sarria in the early morning mist, the Camino passes the convent and heads through the old town and down to the Rio Celeiro, where we cross the medieval Ponte Aspera (Rough Bridge), so named because it was constructed using roughly cut stones. The mist creates a beautiful and magical atmosphere, which at the same time is sombre and surreal. We are quiet and protected in our shroud.

Gradually the mist clears from the higher ground, and is left hugging the valley floor. Surrounding hills protrude like islands in a white sea.

The sun becomes stronger, the sky so blue. We are visiting the Romanesque Igrexa Iglesia de Santiago at Barbadello. Its ancient lichen-covered stone crosses and tall, square bell tower glow in the morning light. An old priest greets us and we sign a visitors' book, amazed at the number of nationalities who have been here before us. The priest stamps our Pilgrim's Passports and offers us his hand. It is soft and warm; his face is gentle and kind.

The church is dark and austere inside, yet sensitive in its simplicity. Outside we study the simple tympanum over the entrance. We walk past the stacked stone burial tombs which form the outer wall surrounding the church — some are ancient, some new.

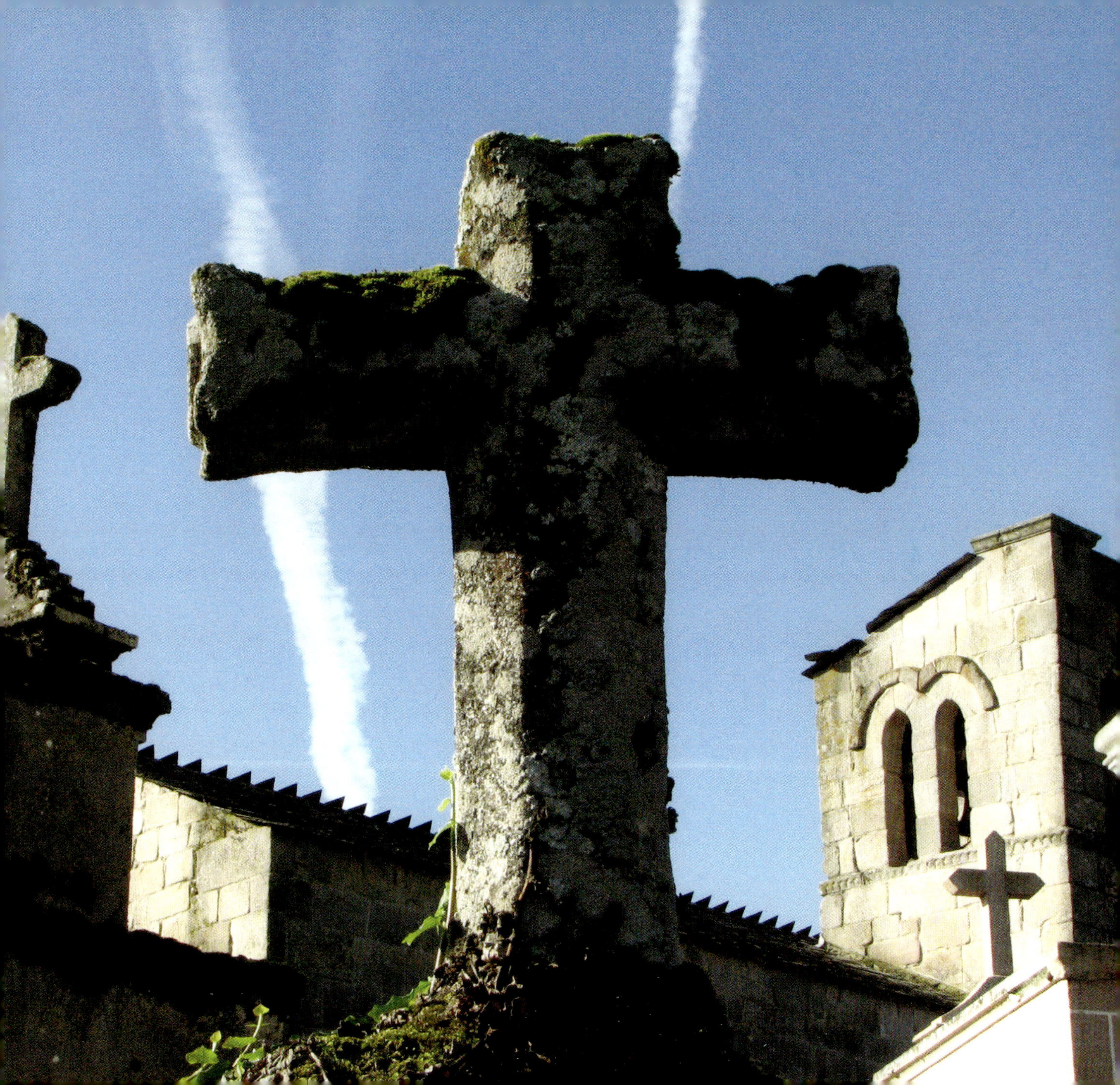

Passing the 100 km waymarker to Santiago de Compostela is a special moment. Messages are left here by pilgrims to mark this symbolic point of their journey.

Other items are left too!

Horreos are traditional storage bins for grain, mainly corn. This one is modern, but many, particularly in the Galicia region, have been built for hundreds of years, all following a similar design — rectangular, made of stone, resting on stilts or solid blocks, with a pitched roof and topped with crosses. They store the grain free of humidity and out of reach of hungry rodents.

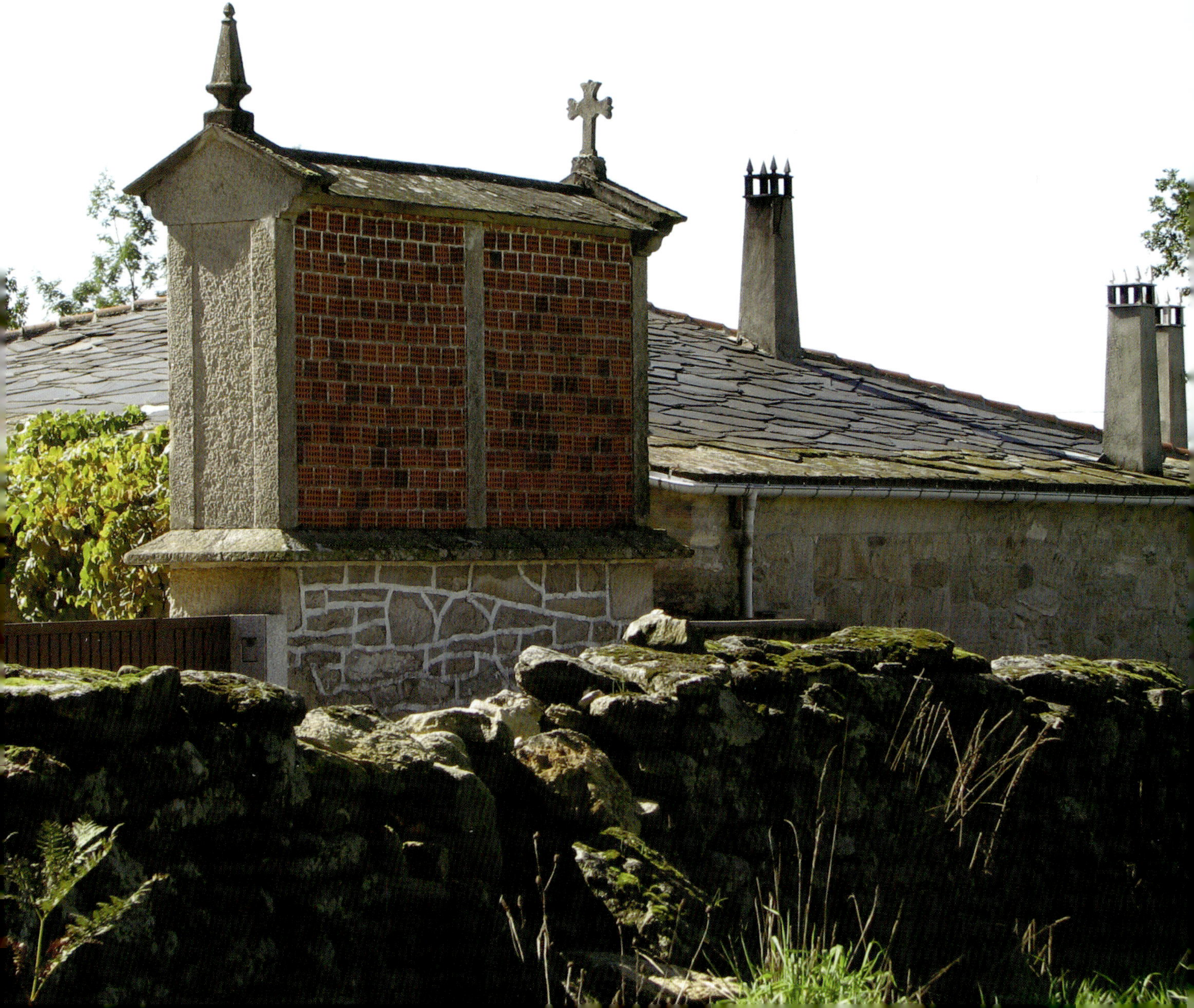

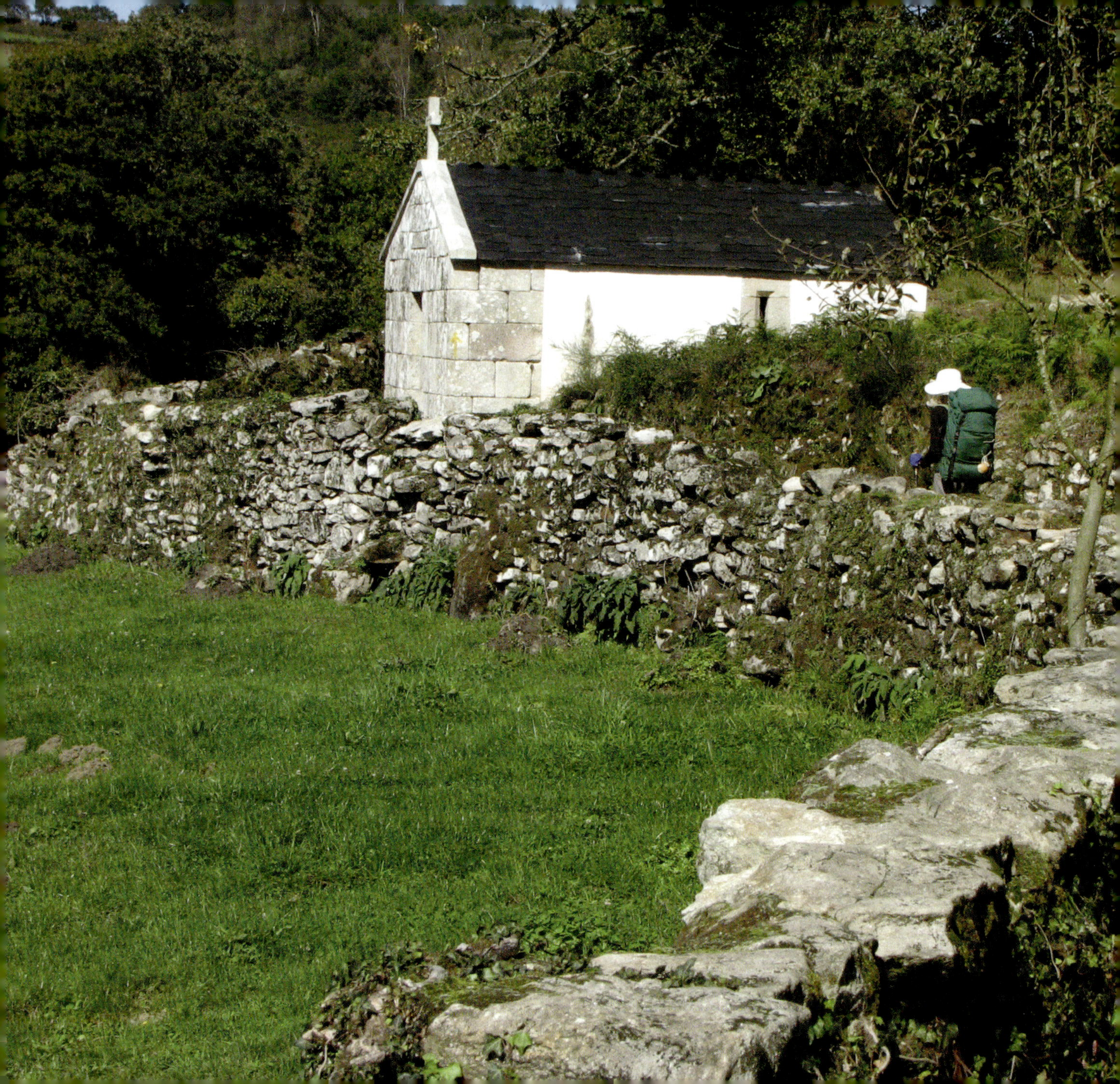

Walking from Sarria to Portomarín is 'a day of all days'. The early morning mist softly and slowly clears into a bright sun-filled day.

We walk along wonderful cool tree-lined pathways, shaded by huge ancient oaks and chestnut trees. The high rainfall of this region makes the countryside green and lush … and sometimes very muddy underfoot.

In the numerous hamlets and tiny collections of well-kept farms and outbuildings, there is lots of activity; tractors in use, cows being milked or herded along the Way, fruit being gathered from overladen apple trees, ripe chestnuts being collected and grain being stored in the *horreos*.

There is a soft rhythm about today's walk. It is a contemplative spiritual day, a day to look inward and reflect on this ancient pilgrim path, to live in the now and to be thankful for every part of this experience.

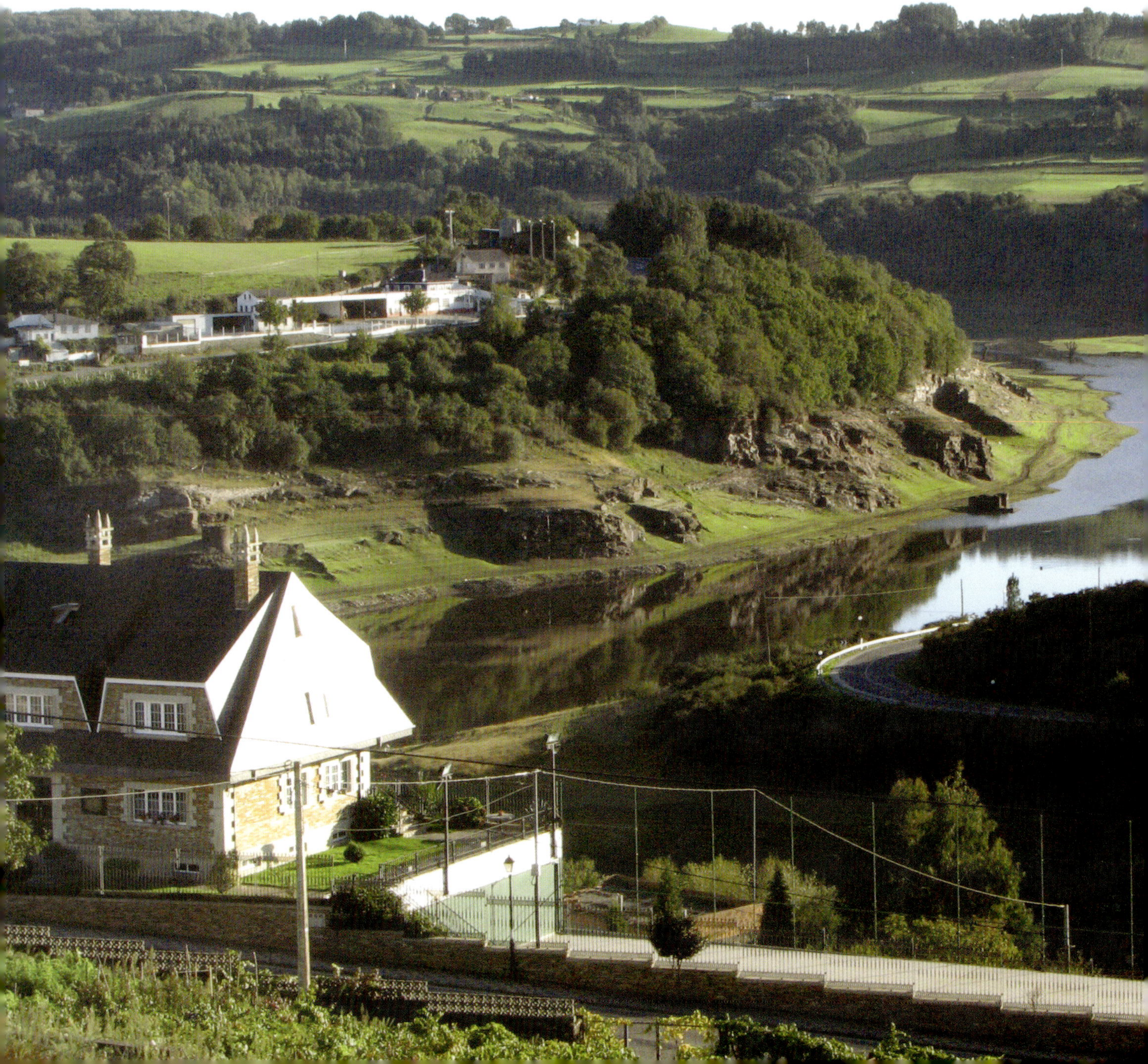

Portomarín was redeveloped on the northern bank of the Belesar Reservoir after its creation in 1962 when the old town was flooded. Many of the buildings, or parts of buildings, from the old town were rebuilt stone by stone, including the 13th century Iglesia de San Nicolas, also known as the Iglesia de San Juan, which dominates the *plaza*. It has an impressive and colourful rose window and interesting carved portals. The town was the fortified headquarters for the Knights of San Juan of Jerusalem.

An ancient Roman stone bridge connected the northern district with the southern district, which had links to the Knights of Santiago and the Knights Templar. The bridge created a strategic divide between these orders during a turbulent time. Destroyed in the 12th century, it was later reconstructed, with stairs leading onto a cobbled main street flanked by stone colonnades into the main *plaza*. When the dam is low, the ruins of the old town can be seen, as well as the ancient bridge, upon which the modern one is built.

We book into a pension, take off our backpacks and enjoy our view overlooking the dam waters at Portomarín. Outside the window bees are buzzing around a flowering bush, the hills are sparkling and green, and the forests are thick down to the water's edge.

In the restaurant downstairs we experience a delicious end to our wonderful day's walk, sampling some of Galicia's delicate whites and fine reds, accompanied by a basket of sliced *panecillo* (small round loaves of bread).

With fishing Galicia's mainstay, there are many seafood choices on the menu — octopus (*pulpo*), steamed and dusted with paprika is a favourite, as are the shellfish. The Galicians also enjoy cooking with meat, and there are thick hot soups, rich vegetable and meat dishes. They offer, too, great cheeses and a tasty quince jelly. For dessert we enjoy the famous almond tart of Santiago.

TO PALAS DE REI

The Camino is not always a quiet tree-lined path, passing misty cloud-filled valleys or crossing rushing streams. On our way to Palas de Rei we have to walk beside a long stretch of road, sharing our journey with many trucks and cars. It is noisy, as are the increasing number of pilgrims passing us.

We have time to play with our shadows — great long shadows created by the early morning sun at our backs stretch way out before us, teasing us to catch up. A poem by Robert Louis Stevenson comes to mind about a child who had a shadow who 'liked to grow', and would 'sometimes shoot up taller like an India-rubber ball'.

There is also time to appreciate the really small things along the way: droplets of water resting on spider webs and sparkling like diamonds, flowering bushes along the road's edge.

Finally the road quietens, the traffic lessens. A lovely misty valley appears on our left, revealing green rolling hills and woodland once more.

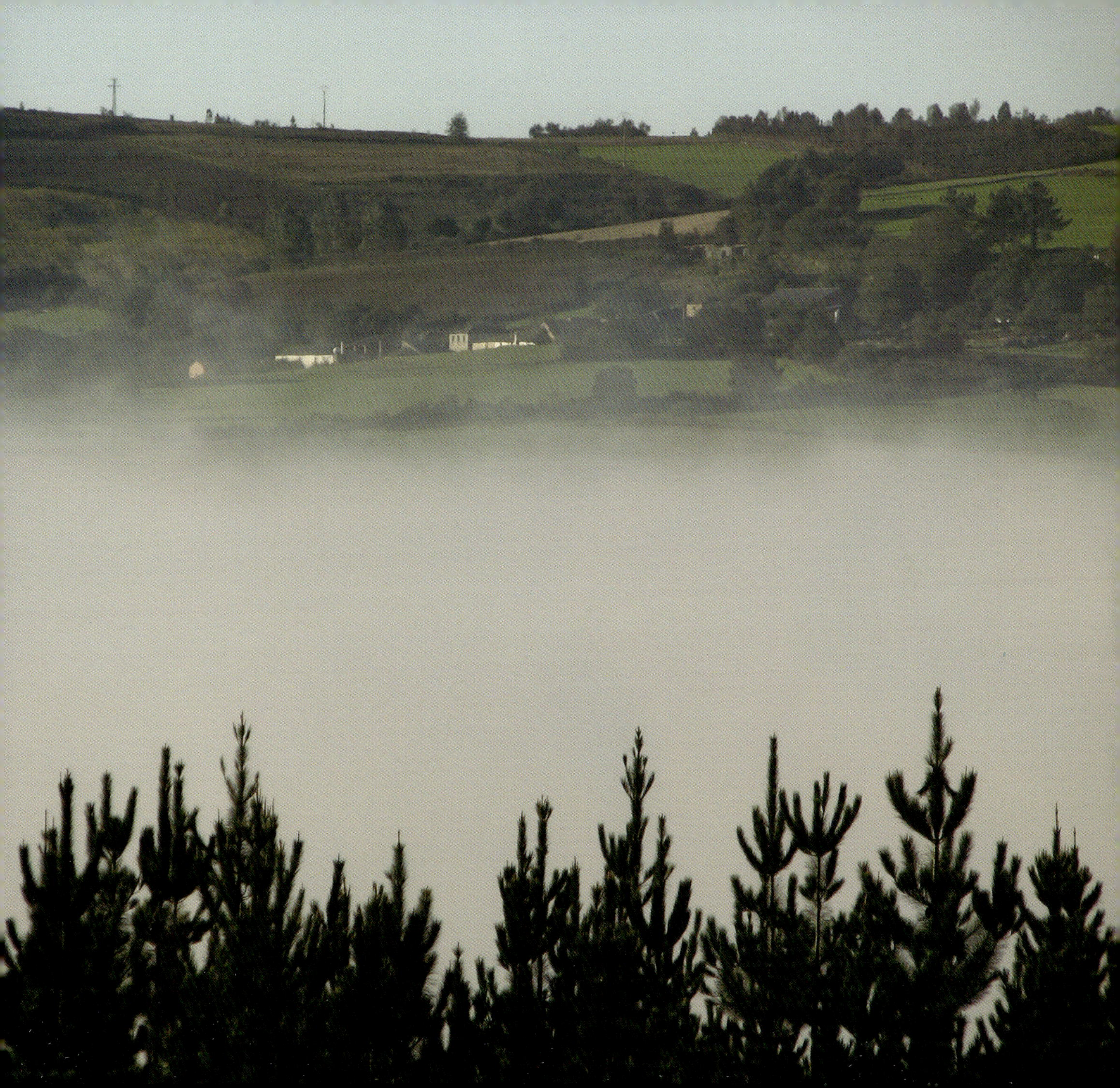

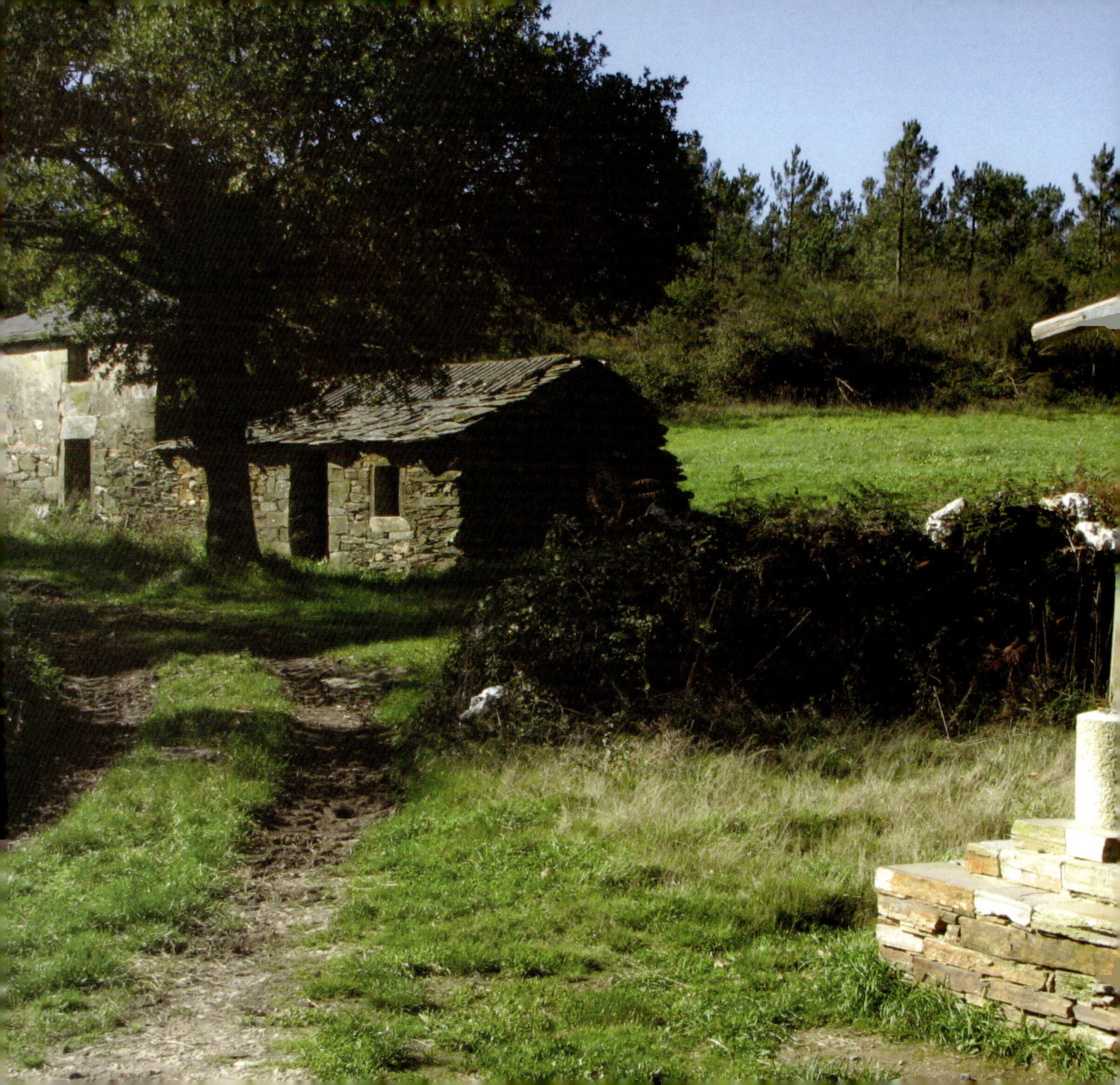

In the small hamlet of Castromaior we pass the lovely Romanesque church of Santa Maria. Further on, at the entrance to an abandoned stone farmhouse, a very simple yet powerful wooden cross marks the Way.

In the 9th century this area was a scene of bloody battles between Moors and Christians. Now it is peaceful farming country.

It is warm and sunny. We stop at an enterprising farm which serves meals, and eat our lunch on a sheltered deck overlooking the gently rolling hills. A tiny 12th century church looks down into the valley where the mist is still slowly rising. Ancient and new burial tombs abut the maize fields. This is a serene and beautiful place in which to pause and absorb a moment in time; a quiet spiritual place where all is still.

Continuing, we pass an interesting 17th century wayside cross made of granite and covered in lichen. Carved at its base is a relief depicting the crucifixion of Jesus. An ancient oak provides a shady place to rest.

There is much activity in the small village of Eirexe, but as we have seen so many times before, it is mainly the elderly who are caring for the animals or tending to the farms.

Despite being warned to be wary of dogs, we find that the dogs we pass are completely uninterested in us. Maybe they are tired of seeing so many pilgrims pass by.

A delightful garden café out of Portos, not far from Eirexe, is a welcoming place to rest and enjoy a coffee before setting out on the 4.6 km detour to the small hamlet of Vilas de Donas and its simple Romanesque granite church built in the 13th century as part of an older monastery complex established for nuns (*donas* means 'women'). Dark and haunting within, it has a richly carved portal, stone effigies and tombs of the Knights of the Order of Santiago, complete with their coats of arms, and paintings of Christ and others, including female figures covering the walls. It is another jewel of the Camino.

If the detour makes the day's walk too long, a taxi can be arranged from the café.

After the detour another hour's walk leads us down the busy main street of Palas de Rei ('Palace of the King'), a street lined with shops, restaurants, places of accommodation and an interesting church with a Romanesque portal. Once a town inhabited by Visigoths, Celts and Romans, today there is little evidence of a palace or its historical past for the pilgrim to explore.

Heading out of town the next day, the yellow arrows marking the Way are reassuring and welcoming. They appear regularly, painted on roads, buildings, fences, stone markers and wooden signs — anywhere which provides good visibility to the approaching pilgrim. They make the life of the self-guided walker easier.

We nevertheless did miss the sign indicating a detour to the manor house of Palacio Villamayor de Ulloa and the Castillo Pambre. The detour forms a looped circuit from the main route and we were told it was worth a visit despite the extra couple of kilometres. The manor house is well maintained, and the 14th century castle is very impressive with its four corner towers and inner keep still standing.

TO ARZÚA

The walk from Palas de Rei to Arzúa is very beautiful, as the Way attempts to keep its distance from the noisy main road. We find ourselves crossing many rivers, walking through cool, shady woodlands of gnarled oak trees, and through small ancient villages that appear almost one on top of each other. The early morning sun backlights the trees, turning the leaves the brightest of greens and creating a speckled effect against the darkness of the shade. The air is cold and crisp.

An early stop for a warming cup of coffee is greatly appreciated. We can feel the excitement among walkers who are eager to reach Santiago de Compostela. Our feelings are mixed: we look forward to Santiago, but are saddened at the realisation that our journey will soon end. The Way has become a friend, and we have found a rhythm as we walk, our mind and body stripped of all but what is essential, teaching us about a much simpler life in the present.

The narrow old grain *horreos* still fascinate us, and we notice variations in the way they are constructed. This one has been built on large stone benches atop a stone fence. Others are freestanding. Some have slate roofs, others tiled. Made of wood or stone, some are decorated with Christian crosses, some with ancient symbols .

The sun creates shadows across the path, magically drawing us forward. It is so beautiful we wish we could walk forever. This has to be heaven.

TO ARZÚA   131

It is a long weekend, the sun is shining, it is warm and there is no rain — unusual for Galicia, as this region is renowned for its rain.

The fine weather brings out the locals — we see people outside Furelos gathering hay and spreading out corn to dry in the sun before storing it in the open *horreo*. Others are gathering mushrooms and drying chestnuts. It is October and autumn is the time to store for winter.

As we draw near to Santiago there are many cafés, taverns and various types of accommodation in the countryside to cater for the increasing number of walkers and bike riders. There are also more unsightly scrap yards and modern industrial estates.

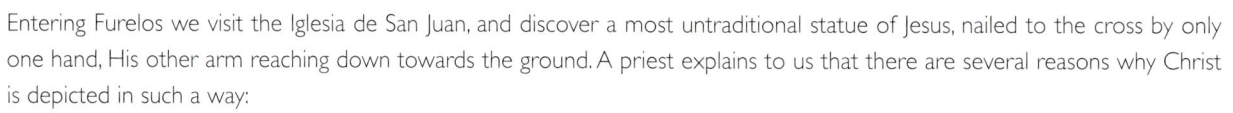

Entering Furelos we visit the Iglesia de San Juan, and discover a most untraditional statue of Jesus, nailed to the cross by only one hand, His other arm reaching down towards the ground. A priest explains to us that there are several reasons why Christ is depicted in such a way:

> Jesus the Christ crucified who through His cross links the absolute of His life to us on earth, His arm reaches down to the foot of the cross where we are on earth, His hand held full of love and tenderness for us.
> It shows the merciful love of Christ for mankind and His extended hand towards earth consoles us.
> It is a perfect bridge between heaven and earth.
> It is a point of union with God the Father, Jesus the Divine and us on earth. Jesus is called to eternity and survives.

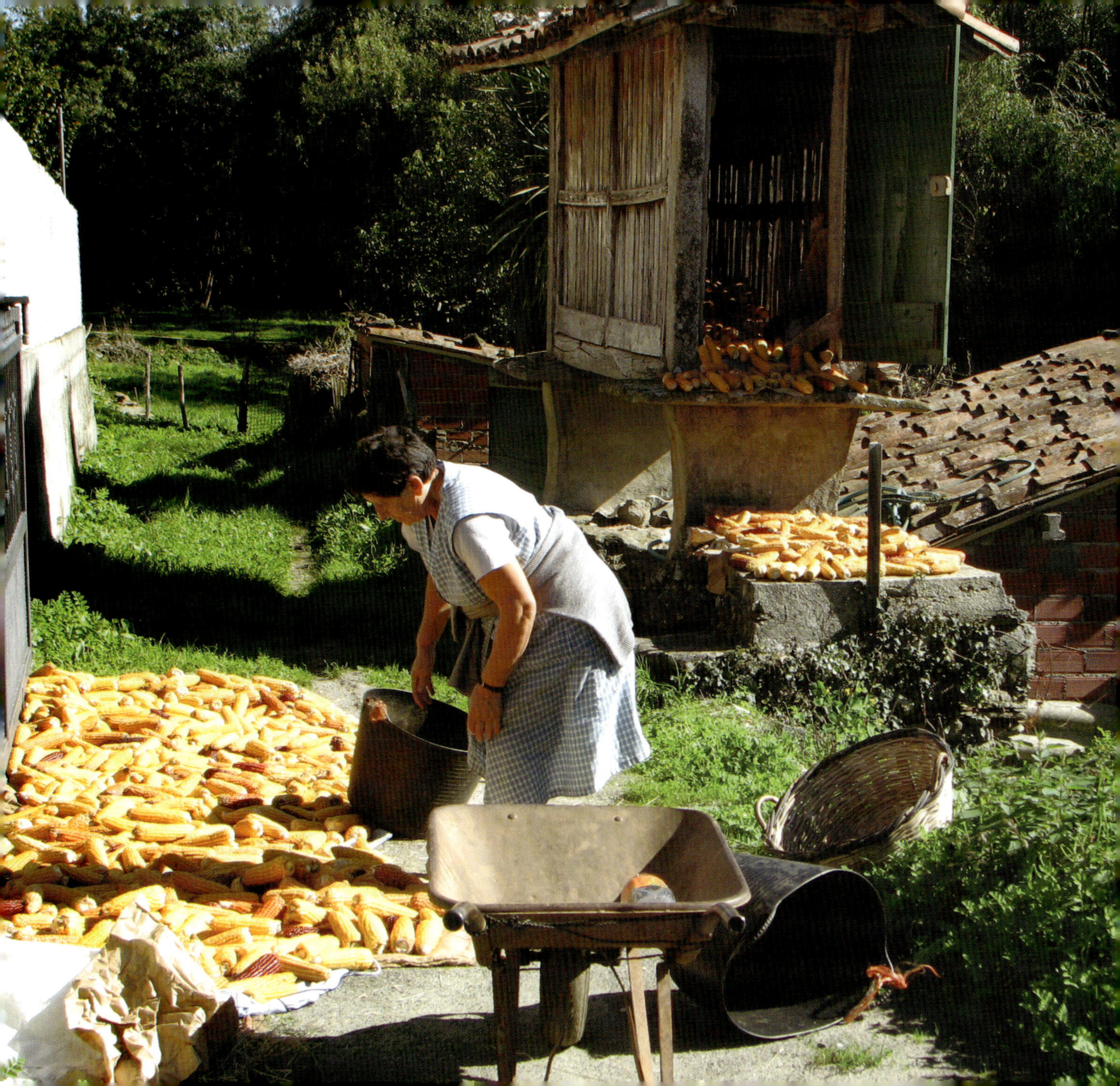

A typical *albergue privado* (private hostel).

Walking on from Furelos we enter the modern suburbs of Melide, a town which dates back to pre-Roman times. In its old quarter we find the most ancient stone *cruceiro* (cross) in Galicia, dating back to the 14th century. These carved granite crosses marked the Camino in medieval times. There are ancient churches and buildings in the square, and in the monastery there are interesting 15th century frescoes depicting St James the Moor-slayer, the Warrior.

The popular family-run restaurant of Exequiel which specialises in *pulpo*.

We are, however, keen to reach a restaurant on the way into Melide, called Exequiel, which is known for its Galician specialty, *pulpo* (octopus). The restaurant is buzzing, its large barn-like area filled to the brim with locals and some pilgrims sitting on benches at long wooden tables. Large pots are boiling and being stirred. Grandma is chopping, her daughters are cooking and young boys are running as they deliver wooden platters of cooked *pulpo* and bread to the tables. House wine is supplied in red jugs, and poured into small red ceramic bowls.

There is hardly a spare place to sit. Seeing our dilemma, four Spaniards beckon us to join them at their table. We are thrilled to learn that they are on the Camino, riding their bikes for one week to Santiago. They have dark sparkling eyes and wondrous smiles and help us order our food and more jugs of the local wine.

Using toothpicks we secure our pieces of *pulpo*, which is delicious and bright with its sprinkling of paprika. The wine is dry, cold and refreshing and the bread smells so good. Despite our meagre Spanish and their equally poor English, we share a great camaraderie, a common bond created by the Camino. All about there is much chatter and laughter, it is infectious.

We leave Melide through the old quarter, and now our path meanders through lovely forests, undulating as it crosses clear bubbling streams. Small hamlets slip by, one by one.

After our delightful lunch there is no time to find or take the detour north of Melide to visit the monastery of Santa Maria of Sobrado which dates back to the 10th century and was built mainly by Cistercian monks sent from France in the 12th century. It eventually fell into ruin until 1954 when the Archbishop of Santiago de Compostela and the Cistercian Order took on the task of saving the monastery. In 1966 Cistercian monks returned to live there.

The Cistercian Order is very austere and follows the literal observance of the Rules of St Benedict. It believes in the value of manual labour: 'You are only really a monk when you live from the work of your hands'.

Further on is the village of Boente and the Igrexa Santiago, where James is depicted not as a pilgrim or a warrior, but as a saint. To our right is Castañeda, where the pilgrims deposited their limestone rocks carried from Triacastela.

A beautiful walk to Arzúa. The forests of eucalypts are very familiar to us as Australians; the small hamlets and clear bubbling streams so delightful. Although the main road interrupts our peaceful route several times, the path manages to follow a quieter Way.

The sense of excitement is mounting and there is a more hurried pace, an impatience, by some of the walkers and bike riders.

The old quarter of Melide.

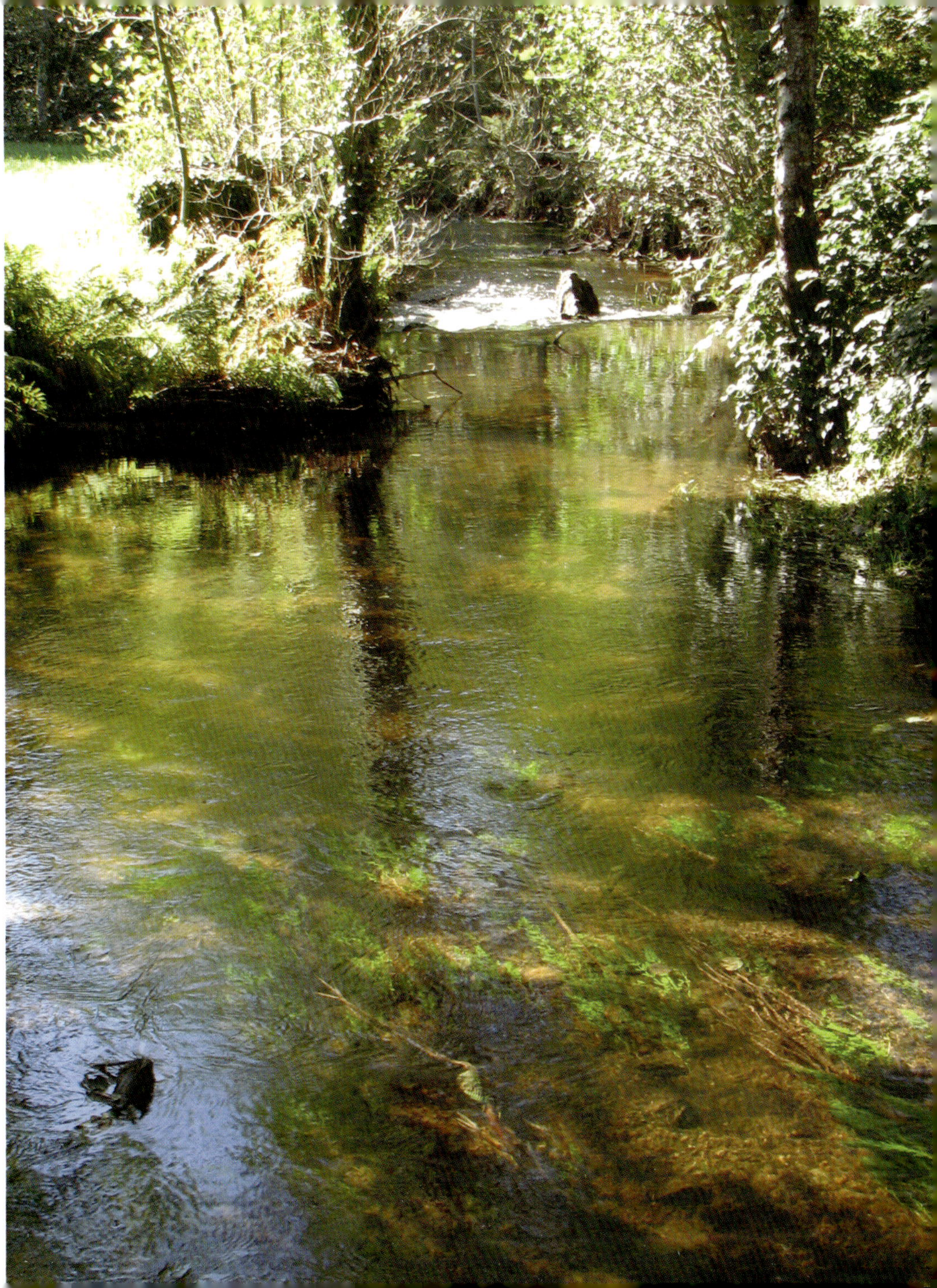

TO ARCA

From Arzúa to Arca we walk through picturesque farming country with gentle rolling hills. The gradient is easy.

Our last night on the Camino. We stay at a very attractive hotel built on the outskirts of Arca. Our window looks out onto fields of fruit trees, corn and small farmlets. There is a backdrop of eucalyptus trees.

We join familiar pilgrims for a walk around this small village which sits on the busy main road to Santiago and is the threshold of our final day's walk.

There are some wondrous old stone buildings, resplendent with armorial shields. We are again amazed at the way huge blocks of stone are used in their construction. Even in the simplest of farmhouses, the workmanship of the stonemasons who quarried, carted and cut the stones to build the walls which have lasted so long is awe-inspiring.

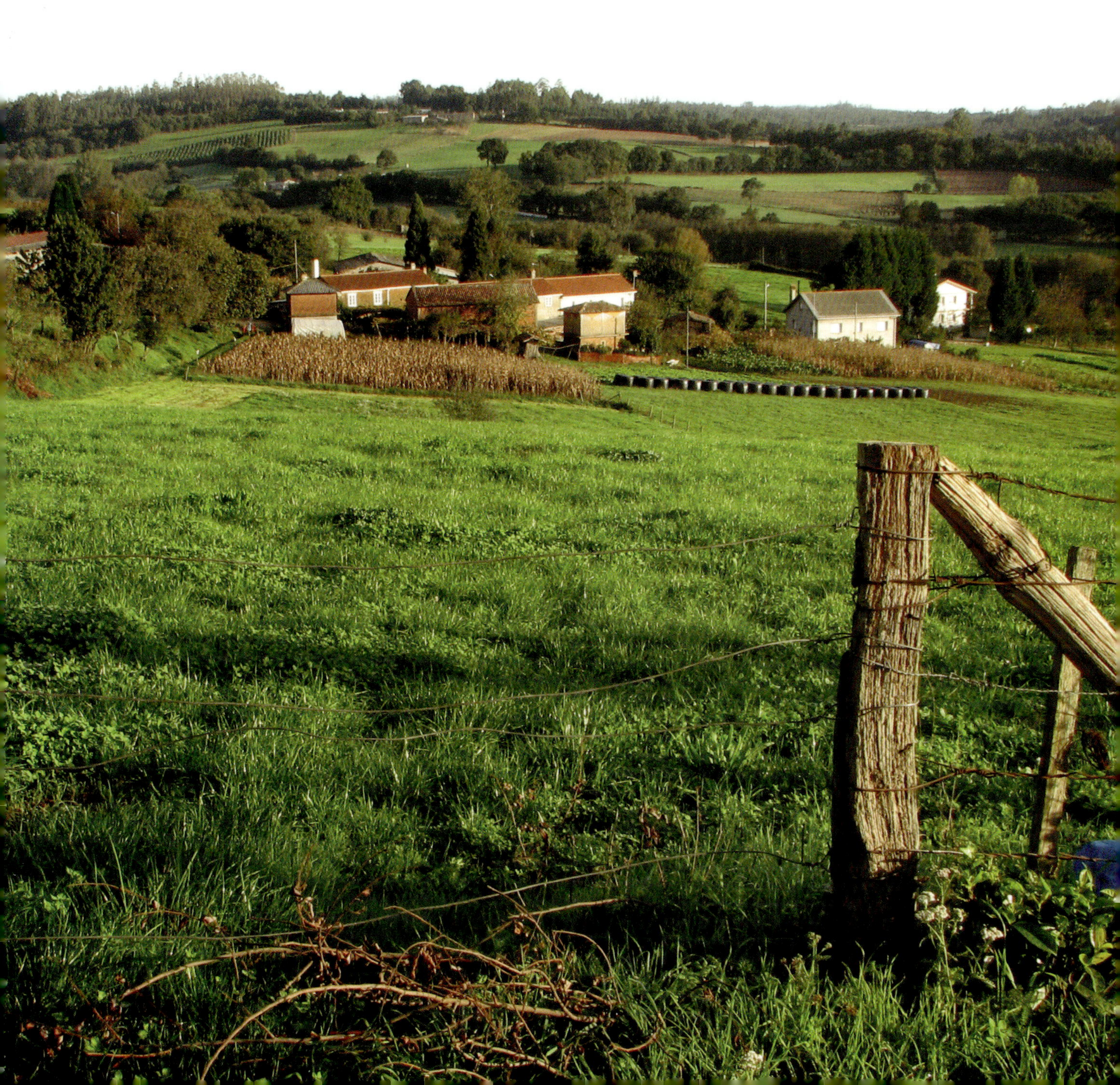

We pass *horreos* full of corn for winter, and fat, well-cared-for cattle being returned to their barns for the night.

TO SANTIAGO DE COMPOSTELA

At the boundary marker on the outskirts of the city.

Our last walking day on the Camino is overcast and light rain is falling. Our excitement builds at the thought of nearing Santiago and encourages us to walk too fast. The peaceful eucalyptus forest with its sprinkling of flowers in the undergrowth tries to settle us.

We pass the airport on the outskirts of Santiago. There is more noise. More traffic. More people walking and riding bicycles. The familiar waymarkers indicate how little there is left to walk.

The journey has been a friend, a timeless journey of self discovery, offering us a chance to reflect, away from our everyday life, to strip away the non-essentials and live freely and simply. We cross the Rio Lavacolla where medieval pilgrims would cleanse and purify themselves before entering Santiago de Compostela. Today the waters are dirty, and instead of participating in a traditional wash, we stop for a warming cup of coffee at a local café.

With just over 4 km to go the route climbs slowly up to Monte Gozo (Mount of Joy), at the top of which there is a modern statue. From here pilgrims used to catch their first glimpse of the cathedral's spires, but today the view has changed — the high ground is now surrounded by buildings, including a large sports stadium and an 800-bed *albergue* on the slopes. Only the small chapel of San Marcos adds any sense of history to this pilgrim's lookout. A huge storm approaches and we arrive in Santiago during a downpour, the heaviest we have experienced along the Way.

SANTIAGO DE COMPOSTELA

WE MADE IT — joyous and happy at arriving in Santiago and completing our Camino. It is an emotional time reaching our destination and we reflect on how important the journey has been, for it is 'the journey, not the arrival, (that) matters' — T. S. Eliot.

Arriving in the old quarter, we leave our backpacks at our hotel and make our way towards the cathedral. We greet and embrace our fellow pilgrims, bonded by the Camino and by reaching Santiago.

The thrill at seeing the cathedral's spires rising above the buildings at the end of the narrow streets is almost overwhelming. We are torn between rushing towards it and just savouring the moment. We decide to take our time and visit the nearby Pilgrims' Office, on the first floor in the old Casa do Deán, and apply for our Compostela. Originally a priest would interview every pilgrim who applied, but now the very helpful staff assist us in filling out our declarations and validate our Pilgrim's Passports. Our certificates, worded in Latin, are written out — names are translated whenever possible.

With our names listed to be read out at the midday mass in the cathedral the next day, the formalities are complete. Our Compostelas are safely rolled into a cardboard cylinder and placed in our daypack.

We sit on the steps before the cathedral's magnificent western façade, overlooking the Obradoiro Praza. Looking down upon us from his niche high in the central tower is St James, dressed as a pilgrim. Our footsteps, like so many others, have made the journey on the Camino and delivered us safely to Santiago de Compostela, the resting place of St James.

To see the cathedral for the first time with its tall, dominating western façade is wonderful and exciting, but also overwhelming. Many days are needed to explore, to unravel its layout, to walk through its many *prazas (plazas),* to visit its numerous chapels and museums, to marvel at its detailed reliefs and statues. There is a warm sense of spiritual belonging as the cathedral becomes more familiar.

Despite our preparation and research, we were unaware that our journey could be so powerful; that we would be so totally immersed and carried along. As John Steinbeck says in *Travels with Charley*, 'we do not take a trip; a trip takes us'. We feel wonderfully content yet excited to continue our journey and allow it to take us on through this marvellous cathedral rising behind us.

We made it!

We are drawn into exploring the four *prazas* surrounding the cathedral. The most famous and most beautiful is the large Obradoiro Praza, the heart and soul of Santiago and a place of constant activity.

The word *obradoiro* means 'workshop' in Galego: this was where the stonemasons worked during the cathedral's construction. The Baroque façade was built in the 18th century to protect the rich Romanesque 12th century Portico de Gloria which now sits behind the main entrance to the cathedral, at the top of the double staircase. In fact the bulk of the cathedral was built in Romanesque times, back to 1075, with the domes, statues and numerous 'flourishes' coming later. Remains of the original two churches, built in the 9th century, were found within the current cathedral's foundations — as were the old city walls and a defensive tower.

Looking down from the central tower is St James, dressed as a pilgrim.

Some of Santiago's finest buildings surround the Obradoiro Praza. Opposite the cathedral, on the western side of the *praza*, is the Pazo de Raxoi, a splendid French Neo-Classical building from 1764, while on the eastern side is the Hostal de Los Reyes Católicos, built in 1492 by the Catholic monarchs as a pilgrim shelter and hospital; it has a plateresque façade, and is now a *parador*. On the northern side of the *praza* is the Collegio de San Jerónimo, a 17th century building with a re-used medieval front. Originally a school for poor students, it now houses the University Vice-Chancellor's Office. Included in this complex is the Palas de Fonseca, the home of the famous 500-year-old university. Finally, adjoining the left side of the cathedral is the Archbishop's Gothic Palace or Palas de Gelmírez. Gelmírez was Santiago's first archbishop and started building this palace in 1120. The main dining hall with its arched ceilings is wonderful.

Obradoiro Praza — western facade.

Heading right from the Obradoiro façade, around the outside of the cloister, we reach the Praza das Praterías, named after a guild of silversmiths who have occupied the area under the cloister arches since the Middle Ages.

Two façades of the cathedral complex look onto this *praza*. On the left is the plateresque façade of the Treasury, topped in the corner by its tower and completing the cloister. The silversmith shops under the cloister arches open directly onto the *praza*, sheltered by white awnings.

The Praterías façade is the cathedral's only remaining Romanesque façade. It was built from 1100 onwards, with steep steps leading to two arched doorways, above which there are two windows with lobed arches in a Muslim style. Traditionally, this was the entrance for pilgrims arriving from Portugal. Some of the sculptures and reliefs on this façade were brought from other parts of the cathedral, creating a mixture of sizes and styles. A tympanum can be found over each of the entrance doors: the one on the left depicts 'The Temptations of Christ', the on the right the 'Adoration of the Magi' and the 'Passion'.

The Torre del Reloj (clock tower) was built in the 17th century on the right-hand corner of the Praterías façade. As it ascends, its tiers become more slender, delicate, and highly ornamented. The clock face has only one hand, marking the hours. At the top is the Berenguela bell, which rings to announce every hour. It is also where a lantern is lit to guide pilgrims during the Holy Year and on special occasions.

Completing the *praza* directly in front of the Pratería façade is the narrow Casa del Cabildo, built in 1758. In its centre is the striking Fuente de los Caballos (Fountain of the Horses), built in 1829. Interestingly, these horses, which are depicted leaping from the water, have webbed feet.

Turning left off the Praza de Praterías around the base of the clock tower we enter the impressive Praza da Quintana, spectacular for its stone bareness. Divided by a broad sweep of steps into two areas, the upper called Quintana de Vivo (Quintana of the Living), and the lower known as Quintana de Mortos (Quintana of the Dead), it was originally the site of the city's cemetery or necropolis.

The southern side of the *praza* is formed by the Casa de los Canónigos or Casa de la Conga, built in the 18th century. There are now cafés within its colonnades. Directly opposite, on the north side, is the Casa de la Parra, covered in exuberant vegetation.

Opposite the cathedral, and completing the *praza* on its eastern side, sits one of the city's oldest buildings, the Monasterio de San Paio de Antealtares, which dates back to the 9th century. Originally housing Benedictine nuns, it has a stark façade, and a seemingly endless impenetrable wall which features 48 latticed windows. A long stone bench runs along the base of this wall providing a sunny place to sit and relax at the end of the day.

This wider, larger *praza* allows an excellent view of the Torre del Reloj, seen previously from the Praza de Praterías.

The Fountain of the Horses depicts web-hoofed horses leaping from the water.

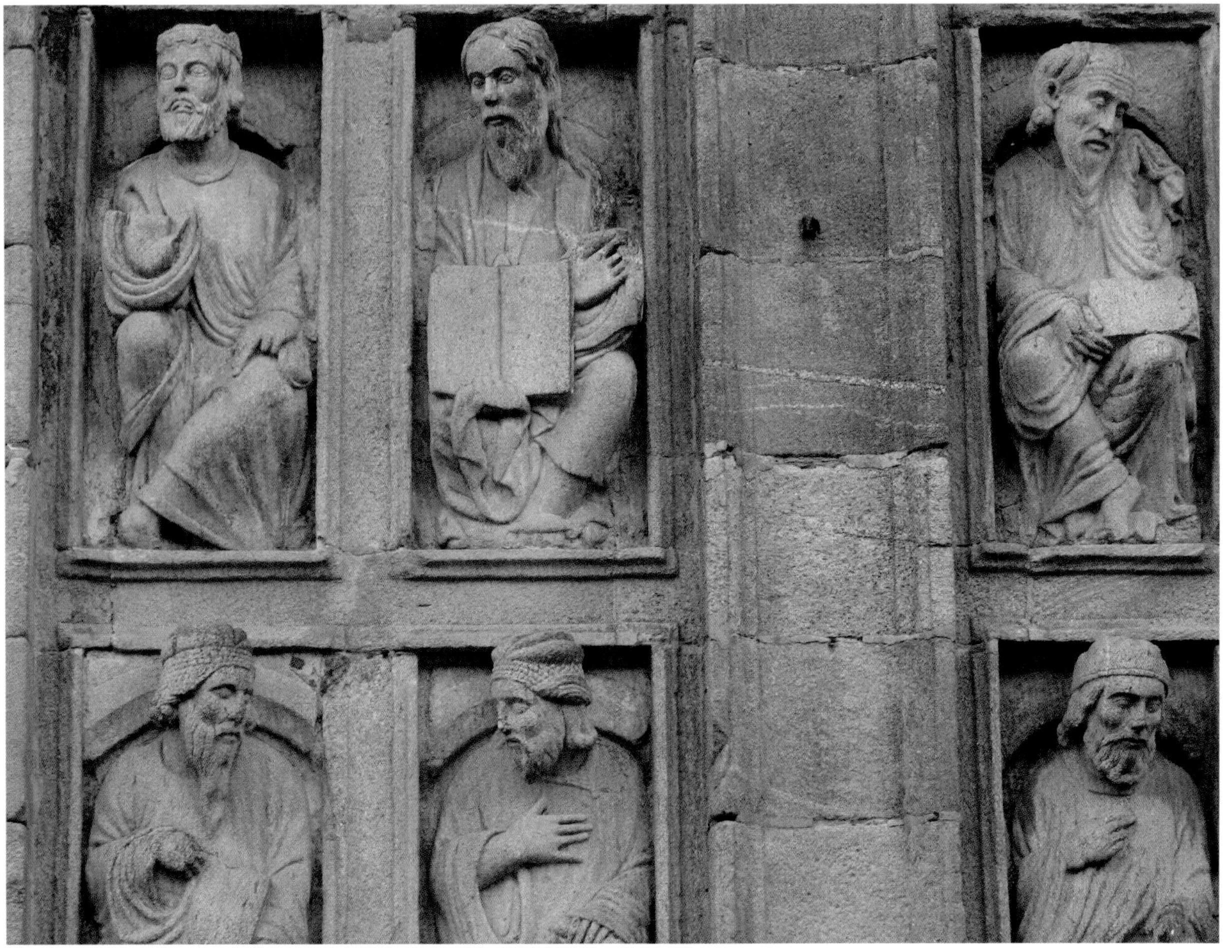

The Quintana façade of the cathedral is the location of Puerta Santa (the Holy Doorway or the Pardon Doorway), which is only opened during Holy Years — one of the most ancient ceremonies of the cathedral.

On 31 December of the year before a Holy Year the archbishop of the city opens the door with three ritual knocks made with a hammer kept in the Treasury Chapel. The third blow of the hammer, accompanied by the phrase, 'Open the doors, the Lord is with us', spoken in Latin, is a signal to knock down the lightweight panels that have sealed the door. The archbishop then removes his mitre, kneels down and recites a Te Deum, an early Christian hymn of praise. The door remains open for the year ahead. In other years the small grated door dedicated to St Pelayo, who discovered the field burial site and tomb of St James, and the Abbots' Doorway on the higher level, provide access from the Quintana façade.

The ceremony of opening the Puerta Santa dates from the 12th century, when the Holy Year was confirmed by a Papal Bull of Pope Alexander III. During Holy Years, many more pilgrims than usual make their way to the cathedral to receive a plenary indulgence — a full remission of sins.

The Holy Doorway is Baroque in style. It has a statue of St James dressed as a pilgrim and flanked by two of his disciples, standing above the Puerta Santa. Reliefs of Apostles decorate each side of the doorway.

Continuing our walk anti-clockwise around the cathedral we turn left into the fourth praza, Praza da Azabachería and the street of the same name, so called because of the famous union of jewellers who still work the beautiful black stone called azabache or jet. Houses used to occupy this area, but due to the risk of fire, it was redesigned in the 16th century. Opposite is the imposing Benedictine Monastery of San Martín Pinario. Covering more than 20,000 square metres, it is one of Spain's largest religious buildings.

Unlike the other entrances, stairs descend from the Praza de Azabachería into the cathedral. The north-facing façade is the most recent of all the cathedral's façades, replacing the earlier Romanesque one with a combination of two styles, Baroque and Neo-Classical. This creates a more modest and restrained façade, and its stonework is now darkened by lichen, giving this side of the church a bleaker atmosphere.

With the cathedral on our left we walk downhill away from the *praza* and connect with the Archbishop's Palace on our right. We walk through the Bishop's Arch, then back into the Obradoiro Praza, where we first sighted the cathedral.

We enter the cathedral through the western façade and the magnificent Portico de Gloria (Entrance of Glory), a masterpiece of Romanesque sculptures and reliefs. The aim of these sculptures was to visually tell Christian stories to the often illiterate churchgoers; they were the pages in a book, each relief telling a tale. Stained glass windows, such as the glorious ones in the León Cathedral, were designed for the same purpose, as storybooks.

The portico and many other parts of the cathedral were built and designed at the request of Ferdinand II of León between 1168 and 1188 by a well-known architect and builder, Master Mateo. His craftsmanship and attention to detail so impressed the Galician poet, Rosalia de Castro, that upon seeing the sculptures he exclaimed, 'Are they alive? They seem to be of stone, those marvellous tunics, those eyes are full of life.'

The portico is made up of three arched entrances into the cathedral. In the middle of the central arch's tympanum is Christ in Majesty, a figure almost three metres high. It shows the wounds on Christ's hands, feet and ribs. He wears a crown and is flanked above by two angels bearing incense. Four Evangelists are placed around him, to the left are a group of the Blessed and to the right are elderly musicians of the Apocalypse. Along the lower edge are angels with instruments of the Passion.

St James is a striking figure in the mullion of the central arch, which is directly below Christ. Almost a freestanding piece, he is dressed as an apostle in a tunic, with bare feet, seated on a cross-shaped chair supported by two lions. His right hand holds a parchment with the words 'Misit me Dominus' ('The Lord sent me'). His left hand leans on a staff with a tau-shaped (cross-shaped) handle. His crown is bronze and inlaid with stained glass decoration.

The central entrance of the Portico de Gloria where Christ sits above St James.

    The Tree of Jesse is below St James. It is a marvellously curved and intricately carved marble column. Known as the human genealogy of Christ, it refers to a passage in the Book of Isaiah and is accepted by Christians as pertaining to Jesus — 'And there shall come forth a shoot from the stump of Jesse and a branch shall grow out of its roots ... ' The sculptures on the upper part of the columns supporting the central arch represent prophets, apostles and others from the Old Testament. The bases of the columns, too, have fantastic animal figures in combat with man. Immediately under the Tree of Jesse is a figure riding two monsters, a symbolic representation of the Patriarch, with the roots of the tree of prophetic visions. Behind the Tree of Jesse, facing into the cathedral, is a kneeling sculpted figure known as Santo dos Croques (the Saint of Bumps or the Saint of Blows). It is said that the statue could be of Master Mateo himself.

Once through the Portico de Gloria the interior opens up into a huge barrel-vaulted main nave, 100 m long and stretching ahead to the main chapel. Built in a Latin cross plan, with a transverse aisle 65 m long, the nave is flanked by aisles which are separated by columns. Galleries run high above the side aisles around the cathedral.

A soft, misty light pervades this space and all who enter there appear very small and insignificant. It is quiet and peaceful.

We are humbled as we approach the heart of the cathedral, the main chapel, with its high altar, shrine and overhead canopy (baldachin) glittering in golden Baroque splendour. The Botafumeiro (the world's largest incense-burner) hangs from the dome over the crossing point of the main nave and the transverse aisle.

The shrine houses the image of St James, who sits gazing down the long main nave to the Portico de Gloria. Above him swirls a cluster of angels and higher still is a statue of St James the Pilgrim. Overhead there is a pyramid-shaped canopy upon which sits a large 13th century statue of St James on horseback — as Warrior and Moor-slayer. The canopy is supported by large figures of angels who stand on twisting Solomonic columns; it is a bright, dynamic, highly decorated and energetic scene.

The remodelling of the main chapel into the Baroque style began in 1659 and took more than 50 years to complete.

Within a substructure of the older 9th century church, under the shrine of St James and the High Altar, is the burial crypt housing the relics of St James and two of his disciples, St Theodorus and St Athananius. The silver casket (reliquary) was designed

The silver casket containing the relics of St James.

by Jose Lasada in 1186 and was placed in the crypt at the end of the 19th century after authentication of the relics by Pope Leo XIII in 1884.

It is fortunate that these relics can be seen at all, because in 1589, in the face of a possible attack by Sir Francis Drake, who was then second in command of the English fleet against the Spanish Armada, the Chapter and Bishop decided to hide the cathedral's treasures, including the relics of the saints. They hid them so well, without leaving any records, that the relics remained lost until excavations unearthed them in 1878.

Upon entering the cathedral, the pilgrim is required to follow certain traditions. The first is to place the fingers of the right hand into the five holes found in the Tree of Jesse and offer thanks for having made a safe journey. So many pilgrims have performed this task over the centuries that these holes have become deep and the marble discoloured. It is hard to comprehend how many have done this before us. The indents are sacred and it is a privilege to touch them. In turn we place our fingers very slowly and carefully into the deep marble holes. The marble is smooth and cold and our fingers linger because of its significance.

The second ritual is to proceed to the Santo dos Croques and touch the head of the statue. By doing this, it is said, the pilgrim will obtain wisdom. It is a demure, small statue, kneeling with hands resting on his chest; curling locks of hair fall to his shoulders, his eyes are closed. We touch his forehead where the marble has darkened from so many other hands and feel a little uncomfortable because the statue's true identity is unknown. If it is Master Mateo, who created so much of this wondrous cathedral, we thank him for his creativity.

The third is to proceed to the right of the high altar and ascend the small flight of stairs to the gold statue of St James, place a hand on his shoulder and tell him why you have made the journey.

Very emotional, we stand behind the magnificent bejewelled statute of St James, hold hands and place our other arms across his broad shoulders, and tell him how special our journey has been. How it developed into something that we had never imagined — overwhelming and totally immersing us both. It is the culmination of our walk, and we quietly thank him for taking care of us on one of the most moving experiences we have ever undertaken.

The fourth ritual is to descend from the high altar and proceed to the reliquary chapel underneath to offer a prayer before the casket containing the relics of St James.

We sit in silence, alone in the small crypt with the silver reliquary shining before us, overwhelmed that we could be in the presence of St James, an Apostle of Jesus who spread His teachings to the pagans in Santiago so long ago.

Throughout these events, St James watches all who pass below, from the central arch above the Tree of Jesse in the Portico de Gloria.

156   SANTIAGO DE COMPOSTELA

The Gothic dome, above the Baroque-style drum and block pulley of the incense burner, is 32 m above the crossing point of the main nave and the transverse aisle. At all pilgrim masses, as well as in the Jubilee (Holy) Years, the Botafumeiro is attached to this pulley system and hoisted by eight red-robed *tiraboleiros (incense carriers)* pulling the rope in unison. The Botafumeiro is guided into a swinging motion higher and higher, until it almost touches the roof of the transept. Built in 1851, it weighs 80 kg, measures 1.6 m in height and when filled contains 40 kg of charcoal and incense. It reaches speeds of up to 60 km/h and dispenses thick clouds of incense, supposedly to fumigate and mask the smell of the hundreds of unwashed pilgrims below.

We witness this amazing spectacle, which has been carried out for more than 700 years, when we attend the midday mass on the second day of our stay in Santiago de Compostela. At this mass, the names of all pilgrims who received their Compostela the day before are read out.

We arrive early, our view is excellent and the seats are quickly filled. Familiar faces appear and pilgrims greet one another with great warmth. We share a proud sense of fulfilment at being present at a mass for pilgrims.

Three elderly nuns from Italy sit in our pew. They do not speak any English but we are united in our excitement. Their faces glow, their smiles are wide and sincere. More and more people are filling every available space. Cameras are clicking.

The Botafumeiro arrives and is set up. The tiraboleiros begin to pull on the pulley ropes and the Botafumeiro begins its upward swing. Higher and higher it travels in an arc from one side of the transept to the other, making a swishing sound as it passes. The crowd quietens, mesmerised.

The nun sitting next to me cannot contain herself any longer and grasps my arm, leading me into the aisle. She holds me tightly, transfixed by the spectacle before us. It is just so special and tears come to her eyes. I am humbled by her emotion.

Stories abound that occasionally the Botafumeiro 'loses its way', however, on this day it swings perfectly.

SANTIAGO DE COMPOSTELA   159

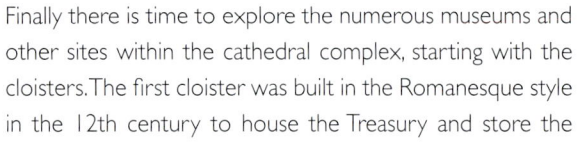

Finally there is time to explore the numerous museums and other sites within the cathedral complex, starting with the cloisters. The first cloister was built in the Romanesque style in the 12th century to house the Treasury and store the cathedral's wealth. This cloister eventually fell into ruins and was replaced by a Renaissance cloister in the 16th century.

In the centre of the cloister there is a large 12th century basin originally installed in the Azabachería Praza by Archbishop Gelmírez. Medieval texts refer to it as the 'fons mirabilis' — it was used by pilgrims to wash themselves before entering the cathedral.

The building that surrounds the cloister houses the treasury, the archive, the chapter house, the library and the museums. We saved the mammoth task of visiting all the museums for our third day. The Botafumeiro is stored in the library when not in use and deserves a closer inspection. A tapestry museum can be found on the upper floor.

There is also an interesting archaeological museum beneath the cathedral, directly off the Obradoiro Praza, and a crypt beneath the Portico de Gloria that was designed by Master Mateo. It has a magnificent central pillar of eight columns which supports spanning arches that create an impressive vaulted ceiling.

Nearby is the wondrous Gelmírez Palace, one of the few surviving examples of secular Romanesque architecture in this region. It was built as a residence for royalty and other important people on their visits to the city. It has a plain façade facing the Obradoiro Praza, but inside there is a fascinating collection of rooms and connecting passageways. Here too are wonderful vaulted ceilings and decorated columns and archways.

SANTIAGO DE COMPOSTELA

FINAL REFLECTIONS

Goethe wrote, 'Europe was formed on the road to Santiago'; what is certain is that the discovery of the tomb of the Apostle James in 815 can be seen as one of the most important events in the Middle Ages. The thousands of pilgrims, particularly during the 11th and 12th centuries, who have walked the Way to Santiago de Compostela have influenced Europe's art and religion, and its economic and cultural life. This influence continued throughout the succeeding centuries and today the pilgrimage is not only full of history, it is still a living, vibrant path.

The city of Santiago de Compostela has preserved the magic of its long history, traditions and spirituality in its buildings, streets and *prazas*. It is an important centre of Christendom, much as Rome and Jerusalem are, and like them, it is a warm and friendly city.

In its centre is the cathedral. It takes days to explore its interior and exterior, to marvel at its artwork, to savour its history, and yet more time is needed to enjoy the city that envelops it so peacefully and engagingly.

Many pilgrims find the energy to walk a further 87 km west to the seaside town of Finisterre, the end of the pagan world; others take a bus for the day to make this journey.

Our stay in Santiago de Compostela was a reflective end to a wonderful walk. It gave us time to consider what the walk meant to us and the ways in which it will remain within us and be part of our continuing journey.

For many, the Camino is undertaken with a clear purpose, as a time to come to terms with many crossroads, whether personal, emotional or spiritual. To others it is a challenge in terms of fitness and stamina and achieving a goal. For whatever reason the Camino is undertaken, the journey is what matters and the common bond formed among the pilgrims was one of the most rewarding aspects of the experience.

May your Camino footsteps — your pilgrimage — allow you to uncover the riches that ancient places can bring and discover their power, for it can become an inward and an outward journey, a liberating journey allowing you to let go and giving you the freedom to sing, dance, praise and love. Have a buen camino, a good walk, through the pages of this book, or by venturing onto the Way.

CAPITULUM hujus Almae Apostolicae et Metropolitanae Ecclesiae Compostellanae sigilli Altaris Beati Jacobi Apostoli custos, ut omnibus Fidelibus et Peregrinis ex toto terrarum Orbe, devotionis affectu vel voti causa, ad limina Apostoli Nostri Hispaniarum Patroni ac Tutelaris **SANCTI JACOBI** convenientibus, authenticas visitationis litteras expediat, omnibus et singulis praesentes inspecturis, notum facit: *Dnum Malcolm Iacobum Wells* hoc sacratissimum Templum pietatis causa devote visitasse. In quorum fidem praesentes litteras, sigillo ejusdem Sanctae Ecclesiae munitas, ei confero.

Datum Compostellae die *16* mensis *Octobris* anno Dni *2006*.

Canonicus Deputatus pro Peregrinis

The official Compostela certificate is worded entirely in Latin.

PLANNING AND PHOTOGRAPHY HINTS

WHEN TO GO

The spring months (March and April) are recommended for those who prefer tranquillity. There are fewer pilgrims, good walking weather and spring flowers. However, it is likely to be cold and rainy in the mountain areas, especially in Galicia. We walked in autumn (September and October), when the number of pilgrims equals the spring average, and found the temperature ideal, at around 18°C to 22°C. July and August can be extremely hot, especially on the plains. It is also a period with a high pilgrim traffic, accounting for nearly half of the pilgrims arriving in Santiago during a full year. During the Holy Years, falling in July every five years, numbers dramatically increase.

WHAT TO BRING

The most important item to take is comfortable walking shoes. Averaging 23 km a day over a variety of terrains including road walking, they should have strong soles, be lightweight and provide good ankle support. Sandals or lightweight shoes for evenings or sightseeing will give your walking shoes a chance to breathe or dry out.

Reliable rain gear (jacket with good head coverage and rain pants) is also a priority, especially in spring and autumn. Also ensure your backpack is waterproof with a cover and inner liner. A broad brimmed hat and sun cream are essential. It is important to keep your backpack light and have it correctly adjusted so that the weight is carried on your hips and not your shoulders. We managed to cull our backpacks down to 9 kg each. The use of ski poles is recommended as they reduce the impact on your body by up to 25% if you use them properly.

Dress in layers. The wool garments currently available are excellent. Of different weights they can be worn in various seasons with many styles ranging from T-shirts (short-sleeve and long-sleeve), to jumpers and jackets. The wool is easy to wash, dries quickly, does not crush, is lightweight and not bulky. It also whisks away moisture from the skin. Pure wool or wool/cotton socks are also recommended — they must be soft so they do not rub and create blisters.

Walking, riding bicycles or horses on the Camino.

We managed on two outfits per day, one for walking and the other for town wear, each being interchangeable when required (with a couple of extra T-shirts tossed in). A nylon line and a few clothes pegs are handy.

As there are many drinking fonts along the Way (less across the plains) and the water is safe, one-litre water bottle each is sufficient. It is important to be aware of where the fonts are located and drink plenty of water to avoid dehydration.

Before leaving St Jean Pied de Port we posted our excess baggage ahead to the Santiago Post Office. It was an excellent and reliable service. Additionally, backpacks can be transported to the next night's accommodation — information about companies available to do this varies from town to town and needs to be validated. A smaller and lighter daypack in which to carry essential daily items is required to replace the backpack.

WHERE TO STAY

Accommodation is varied along the Way. Top of the range are the *paradors*, five-star converted pilgrim hospitals or monasteries, mostly found in the larger towns. They can be very grand. Beneath this level there is a wide range of hotels, down to hostels and pensions, with or without private bathrooms.

Pilgrim *albergues (pilgrim hostels, refuges, inns)* are every 10–20 km along the Way (not as plentiful on the plains) — approximately 80 are located along the Camino de Santiago. They are run by parishes, local governments or by private owners, and provide dormitory-style bunk-bed accommodation — a sleeping bag is recommended as most do not supply sheets or blankets. The number of beds offered varies from 10 to more than 100. There are communal bathrooms, and some have communal kitchens, pay telephones, laundry facilities, internet services and occasionally central heating and single rooms. Their size and standards vary; some were pretty basic and can be very crowded and noisy, so ear plugs are a good idea. Watch out for bed bugs — they are known to be supplied at some free of charge!

Booking ahead is not always possible. Some albergues do not open for bookings until late in the day. While we overnighted mainly in small hotels and pensions, we were impressed by many of the albergues we passed.

An auberge at Barbadello (above) with 18 beds and all facilities, even a caravan set up in the back garden offering coffees and other refreshments. At Arca (below) a hostel with 15 beds and all facilities.

LANGUAGE

Do some work on learning Spanish. A phrasebook is extremely handy. English is not widely spoken in the countryside and even in the larger city hotels it was quite rare to find staff who spoke more than a few words of English.

FIRST AID

Another important item for many walkers is a blister kit, essential to treat 'hot spots' immediately. Support bandages are also helpful for sprains, as are pain relief tablets. In the larger towns chemists (*farmacia*) will assist and most places of accommodation carry their own first aid items.

PHOTOGRAPHY HINTS

Because of the need to keep our overall carrying weight to a minimum, I changed from my trusted Nikon 801S and my favourite 35/135 mm travel lens, both weighing in at 1.5 kg, to a Canon digital 6 mega pixels camera weighing 410 g! With an equivalent auto focus lens of 36–432 mm the camera was more than adequate. A wide angle lens is also extremely valuable.

A waist carry bag 130 x 120 x 140 mm was very handy as it stored the camera, spare batteries, extra memory chips and a tiny 120 mm high flexible tripod.

An international power socket converter is also recommended to allow the use of a battery recharger, along with two sets of NiMH (2500mAh) rechargeable batteries. As a precaution against losing one large memory chip, it is not a bad idea to take several.

REFERENCE BOOKS

Brierley, John, *A Pilgrim's Guide to the Camino de Santiago. Scotland, Findhorn Press Ltd, 2006* (our 'Bible' and guidebook on the walk).

The Lonely Planet 'Walking in Spain'. Victoria, Australia, Lonely Planet Publications, 2003 (there are 37 pages on the Camino walk).

First published 2008 by
FREMANTLE PRESS
25 Quarry Street, Fremantle
(PO Box 158, North Fremantle 6159)
Western Australia.
www.fremantlepress.com.au

Copyright text © Kim Wells 2008
Copyright photographs © Malcolm Wells 2008

This book is copyright. Apart from any fair dealing for the purpose of private study, research, criticism or review, as permitted under the Copyright Act, no part may be reproduced by any process without written permission. Enquiries should be made to the publisher.

Printed by Everbest Printing Co Ltd, China

National Library of Australia Cataloguing-in-publication data

Wells, Kim.

Buen camino: reflections on a journey to Santiago de Compostela / author, Kim Wells; photographer, Malcolm Wells.

North Fremantle, W.A.: Fremantle Press, 2008.

ISBN: 9781921361258 (pbk.)

1. Wells, Kim — Travel — Spain — Santiago de Compostela. 2. Wells, Malcolm — Travel — Spain — Santiago de Compostela. 3. Christian pilgrims and pilgrimages — Spain — Santiago de Compostela. 4. Santiago de Compostela (Spain) — Description and travel. I. Wells, Malcolm.

263.0424611

Photo captions:

Cover: The towns of Azqueta and Villamayor de Monjardín in the distance.

Back cover: Nearing Los Arcos in the Navarre region (left), Santiago Cathedral (right).

Inside front cover: Heading up the Route de Napoleon on the way to Burguete.

Page 2: The pristine, pretty village of Burguete.

Page 4: On a bare hill, a simple wooden cross protectively overlooks the mountain hamlet of O'Cebreiro.

Page 6: Beautiful Pyrenees countryside, near Orisson.

Page 12: The La Quintana facade and clock tower of Santiago Cathedral where St James sits over the Holy Doorway.